A Theology of Atonement
and
Paul's Vision of Christianity

Zacchaeus Studies: New Testament

General Editor: Mary Ann Getty

A Theology
of Atonement
and
Paul's Vision
of Christianity

by
Anthony J. Tambasco

A Michael Glazier Book
THE LITURGICAL PRESS
Collegeville, Minnesota

A Michael Glazier Book published by The Liturgical Press

1   2   3   4   5   6   7   8   9

Library of Congress Cataloging-in-Publication Data

Tambasco, Anthony J.
    A theology of atonement and Paul's vision of Christianity / by
Anthony J. Tambasco.
        p.   cm.
    "A Michael Glazier book."
    Includes bibliographical references.
    ISBN 0-8146-5679-X
    1. Atonement.   2. Atonement—Biblical teaching.   3. Paul, the
Apostle, Saint—Contributions in doctrine of the Atonement.
    4. Bible.   N.T.   Epistles of Paul—Theology.   5. Catholic Church—
Doctrines.   I. Title.
    BT265.2 T25   1991
    232'.3—dc20   91-7112
                                                                          CIP

This book is dedicated with affection to
Phil and Gerri
Mike and Gail
Nicci and Jen

Contents

Editor's Note

Zacchaeus Studies provide concise, readable and relatively inexpensive scholarly studies on particular aspects of scripture and theology. The New Testament section of the series presents studies dealing with focal or debated questions; and the volumes focus on specific texts or particular themes of current interest in biblical interpretation. Specialists have their professional journals and other forums where they discuss matters of mutual concern, exchange ideas and further contemporary trends of research; and some of their work on contemporary biblical research is now made accessible for students and others in *Zacchaeus Studies*.

The authors in this series share their own scholarship in nontechnical language, in the areas of their expertise and interest. These writers stand with the best in current biblical scholarship in the English-speaking world. Since most of them are teachers, they are accustomed to presenting difficult material in comprehensible form without compromising a high level of critical judgment and analysis.

The works of this series are ecumenical in content and purpose and cross credal boundaries. They are designed to augment formal and informal biblical study and discussion. Hopefully they will also serve as texts to enhance and supplement seminary, university and college classes. The series will also aid Bible study groups, adult education and parish religious education classes to develop intelligent, versatile and challenging programs for those they serve.

Mary Ann Getty
New Testament Editor

Preface

This book is the fruit of experience from a number of years of adult education and undergraduate teaching. During that time I have encountered, among other groups, two particular audiences. One group consists of those Catholics who have welcomed the changes in the Church since the Second Vatican Council and have gradually acquired new ways of describing and living their faith. Their roots, however, are in an earlier theology and they are still wrestling with the shift of paradigm and the general overview within which to insert the individual insights that they are developing. I have found that the theology of atonement is a central, paradigmatic concept. In their understanding of why they need Christ, what he does for them, and how he does it, they have a general framework to which they attach much of what they perceive as their vision of Christianity. I have found that frequently these Catholics retain a pre-Vatican II theology of atonement to which they are struggling to reconcile individual post-Vatican II faith insights. When I write later of the popular view of atonement, I am referring especially to the view held by these Catholics. This book seeks to renew the general vision of Christianity and to provide a paradigm of atonement that makes a comfortable setting for theology since the Council.

The other group that I have often encountered are those Catholics who were born after the Second Vatican Council and who have never received in their religious education any adequate framework or paradigm out of which to understand their faith.

Sometimes they have acquired a theology of atonement from their parents, but what they received is a pre-Vatican II theology with the accompanying difficulties mentioned above. This book seeks to give a central vision of Christianity that might help focus the meaning of Christ for Christians after Vatican II. Paul's vision of Christianity will provide the basis, since he lays the foundational and most explicitly articulated theology of atonement in the New Testament.

I would like to express thanks and indebtedness to several people who helped in the writing of this book: to my colleagues Alan Mitchell, S.J., and Leo Madden for their detailed reading of the manuscript and helpful suggestions; to Georgetown University for a sabbatical and reduction in teaching that encouraged the writing. I give special thanks and love to my wife Joan for her enthusiasm and support as the book progressed and for her patience and understanding when the book made intrusive demands on my time and energy.

Introduction

The title of this book needs some explanation. A theology of atonement in its broadest sense describes Christ's saving work in our world, encompassing any explanation not only of what Christ does but also how he does it. The purpose of this book is to show that Paul's vision of Christianity is basically a theology of atonement in this broad sense of the phrase. This study will show that for Paul Christianity is not primarily a set of teachings, nor simply a code of morality or a set of rituals. Though doctrine, morality, and ritual are all important, they are in fact all expressions or consequences of a deeper, dynamic relationship, namely, the action of Christ in our lives. Paul defines Christianity in terms of what Christ does to eliminate sin and to reunite us to God. In this context the "and" in the book's title is to unite the two phrases. Paul's vision of Christianity is a theology of atonement in its broadest sense of describing the goal and the means of Christ's saving work.

Unfortunately, the word "atonement" bears other connotations which are more specific and which raise problems regarding Paul's theology. Unlike the other vocabulary which describes what Christ does for us, "atonement" is the only one that does not evolve directly out of Latin origins but is uniquely English in its history.[1] As it developed in popular usage, it did not embrace all the biblical concepts, but only some. It also incorporated some meaning that diverged from biblical concepts, especially from Pauline the-

[1]For a history of the term, see Robert S. Paul, *The Atonement and the Sacraments* (London: Hodder and Stoughton, 1961) 17–32.

11

ology where the vocabulary of Christ's saving work is most explicitly developed. In this sense, the "and" in the title of this book is to show that there is not only a relationship but also a distinction between what I will refer to as "the popular understanding" of a theology of atonement and Paul's theology as his vision of Christianity. Let us sketch this development and partial divergence in a bit more detail.

At its core "atonement" means "reconciliation"—literally, "at-one-ment"—and suggests the restoration of unity between God and creation. It is a relational word and points to one of the central facts of *what* Christ is all about. In this meaning it draws accurately from Paul: "In Christ God was reconciling the world to himself" (2 Cor 5:19). In its original and, perhaps, most specific and precise meaning, "atonement" should be seen as an equivalent of Paul's word *katallagē,* meaning "reconciliation."

Nevertheless, as the word evolved in English, it carried with it more than just the goal or effect of reconciliation. It implied other ways of describing Christ's saving work. For example, it connotes the cost or effort on Christ's part to purchase or acquire us. In this sense "atonement" would include the idea of redemption, and would still be compatible with Paul, depending on how one understood "cost" or "effort." (Paul says, "You were bought with a price," 1 Cor 6:20.) However, implicit in the popular understanding of atonement is also concern with what I will describe as "the *means* of atonement," associated with theories of sacrifice and legal standing. Atonement came to mean making amends for an offense or offering satisfaction for a wrongdoing or injury. In fact, even more specifically, atonement became associated with a particular theory of sacrifice, which we will consider shortly. In effect, while not losing its ties to the core meaning of "reconciliation" or to a general idea of redemption, it also embraced a further distinct concept, namely, a particular *means* of redemption. Unfortunately, in becoming associated with a specific (sacrificial) means of reconciliation or redemption, atonement included in its meaning some notions that are not faithful to Paul's teaching.

These more specific notions of atonement are common and ingrained in the minds of many Christians, so it is also an important concern of this book to encourage a change in the ideas which are not found in Paul and, in fact, are not biblically based. With this background to the word "atonement" we have, then, the nuances of the title and purposes of this book. We are concerned with showing that Paul's vision of Christianity is a theology of atonement, understood in its broadest sense as any description of the means and goals of Christ's saving work in the world. In doing this, however, we will also keep in mind that there is a common perception of atonement as a particular means as well as goal of that work. We will have to contrast Paul's description of atonement with this popular view. We will concentrate first of all on what I call "the means of atonement," on how Christ achieves his saving work, showing that Paul's ideas are at odds with what I will call "the popular view." Then we will treat Paul's description of what I call "the goal of atonement," of *what* Christ achieves for us. This analysis will lead us to highlight atonement in its most specific meaning of reconciliation and will show Paul's vision as in harmony with that aspect of the popular understanding of atonement. Since, however, Paul uses other ways to describe Christ's saving work, e.g., justification, a theology of atonement in its broadest sense will require that we bring the idea of reconciliation into contact with these other descriptions.

In summary, then, when I treat a theology of atonement, I am describing those ways that Paul talks about Christ's saving work and about *how* Christ achieves that work. I am also conscious that this theology of Paul is partially in agreement and partially in disagreement with a prevalent, popular, and more restricted understanding of atonement. Therefore, I am also interested in showing that Paul's vision of the *means* of atonement is different from the vision of what I call "the popular understanding." His vision of the *goal* of atonement includes the popular and most precise view of atonement as reconciliation, but in a broader sense "atonement" can embrace other ways in which Paul describes the goal of Christ's saving activity, and we will look at some of them.

There is one other concern of this book that needs mentioning, namely, to pay attention to the communal dimensions of Paul's theology of atonement. Recent theology and biblical study have pointed out that religion is too often a privatized and individual concern. Faith has been seen as establishing a purely personal relationship between God and the believer. The recent movements in Scripture studies and theology have been attempts to overcome such limited views of Christian faith and religious experience. There is now a stress on the social and communal dimensions of revelation. In the same way, emphasis has shifted from a purely otherworldly and future heavenly concern to the ramifications of revelation on this world and on the present realities of human existence. Finally, the urgent cries from a world of the poor and oppressed of society have caused us to become more conscious of our previous shortsightedness in reading Paul and other biblical texts. They address new questions and urge us to address new questions to these texts to see what they say about God's concern for social justice. As we look to Paul's theology of atonement, then, we will concern ourselves especially with what Christ's saving action achieves in a world scarred by poverty and oppression.

Prevalent Theory of Atonement

Before we proceed to our study of Paul's theology of atonement, it might be helpful to give a summary description of one model which theology has constructed to explain Christ's saving work and which encapsulates what I have been calling "the popular view today." It is a model given structure and formal definition by St. Anselm at the start of the High Middle Ages, molded out of partial descriptions from earlier traditions.[2] Anselm is the first to construct a formal theology of atonement. There are some debates over whether he is faithful to biblical traditions, and that is what we are going to examine in Paul. In any case, Anselm is probably responsible for the most prevalent of theories about the atonement. I have chosen his model over others because I believe it has been so influential, even if some of the effects today are more conclusions on the popular level or inferences of popu-

---

[2]For a history of the theories of atonement, including Anselm's see Gustaf Aulen, *Christus Victor: A Historical Study of the Three Main Types of the Idea of Atonement* (New York: Macmillan Publishing Co., 1969).

lar thinking and not what Anselm intended. My reconstruction will combine thoughts from Anselm with what I perceive to be consequential common popular conclusions about atonement among Christians today. This will provide a suitable sounding board against which we can discuss Paul's theology of atonement.

Anselm was concerned with showing in a rational argument why Christ had to take human existence and die on the cross. He constructs his argument on certain presuppositions about Scripture, but he wants to speak apart from Scripture so as to be understood by nonbelievers. He begins with the fact that we are in a fallen world and that God faces a world of sin. In this situation God's justice becomes an important factor and, for Anselm, presents only two choices: God either has to punish people or have them offer satisfaction, i.e., make amends for offenses committed against God. Anselm offers a sharp insight in observing that God cannot simply forgive sin, as though it did not matter, and that God must reestablish justice. However, his concepts evoke poor images of God that have been readily taken over by Christians and which form, on the popular level, part of the model that I am reconstructing. God is pictured as judge in a law court or detached setting, and God's justice is pictured as an impartial rendering of verdicts with accompanying rewards or punishments. Again in the popular view God's sense of justice is often tinged with annoyance at best or anger at worst, and God is pictured as saying that men and women must "make up" to divine anger or receive just punishment for sin. Justice is a separate matter from God's mercy, and justice is what prevails in the end!

In asking how persons can make amends or satisfy for sin committed against God, Anselm shows the need for Christ and for the cross. In effect, human beings cannot adequately offer satisfaction for sin, because they can offer only finite satisfaction for an infinite offense. As Anselm explains this, an offense is measured by the one offended and reparation or "making up" is measured by the one making amends. *God* is offended and *human beings* are making amends, so the (finite) satisfaction will never equal the (infinite) offense so as to "cancel" it out. Into this dilemma steps Christ, who is necessary because he is both God and human. As human he can make amends on behalf of humanity, and because he is God, he can offer infinite satisfaction for the infinite offense.

The infinite satisfaction offered by Christ is achieved by his death on the cross because that was an act of obedience which outweighed any of humanity's sinful acts and thereby merited God's reward. Since Christ did not need God's reward, he passed it on to us. Thus, Anselm's model revolves much around a theory of excess meriting, and merit is joined to satisfaction as an essential element of a theory of atonement. Again, on the popular level, Anselm's model was joined to theories of sacrifice and to one in particular whereby Christ's death, more effective than the death of any sacrificial animal, appeased God and thereby satisfied God's sense of justice and thus "made up" for our sins. It is Anselm's theory of merit for satisfaction, as it has passed through this concept of sacrifice to satisfy God's justice, that has been associated more than anything else with the meaning of "atonement" in popular parlance.

In addition to what we said above about the advantages and disadvantages of this model in defining God's justice, we can highlight some further advantages and disadvantages of this model's process itself of satisfying God's justice. On the positive side, it shows the importance of the death of Christ and how serious sin is. On the negative side, the model lacks some elements and again evokes images on the popular level that are not felicitous. For instance, the process of atonement centers only on the death of Christ. It does not show why his life is important, nor does it show how his resurrection is essential as part of the saving process. Moreover, the death of Christ is most often associated in popular imagination with punishment. God takes out on Christ what God should have taken out on us. It is also easy to see how a concept of merit can lead to legalistic views of the process, as does the theory that God's justice has either to punish or to demand satisfaction. At its worst, such an approach situates the entire work of Jesus outside of us as some kind of legal "balancing of the scales," without adequately explaining how we acquire those merits for ourselves or how Jesus radically eliminates sin from our being. Christ seems to do something *for* us, but not *to* us or *with* us. Finally, the model tends to stress personal and individual aspects of atonement and not the social and communal which are of such importance in our time.

Thus we have what I would consider a prevalent theory of atonement functioning in the minds of many Christians today. Some of it is an exaggeration of Anselm's thought. Some of it is the genuine expression of his thought. In any event, the final model underpins what many associate with the meaning of atonement in their lives. We now have our points of comparison for examining what Paul says about atonement.

One final word of introduction: Since we are dealing only with Paul's theology of atonement, we will confine ourselves to those letters which are held by scholars to be certainly of Paul's authorship: Romans, 1 and 2 Corinthians, Galatians, Philippians, 1 Thessalonians, and Philemon.[3] Though there are good arguments that Paul wrote Colossians and a good possibility that he also wrote Ephesians and 2 Thessalonians, we will not base our arguments on these works, though we may allude to them when they confirm a point already made in one or more of the primary seven epistles. Wide consensus is growing that Paul did not author the letters to Timothy and Titus.

[3]Both author and publisher have found the Revised Standard Version of the Bible the most helpful for study purposes and for use in this book. This results in the occasional use of sexist language. For better or for worse, the choice was made to remain faithful to the translation used. The New Revised Standard Version was not available when this book was written. The rest of the book strives for inclusive language.

1

The Justice of God

Much of the popular explanation of a theory of atonement depends on the starting point, namely, prior images of God and God's justice. If God's justice is separated from God's mercy, or if God is seen as rightfully upset or angry with sin, then atonement is readily seen as requiring a "making up" to God or an appeasing of God's anger. It is important, then, to understand clearly Paul's definition of God's justice in order to have an accurate idea of his theory of atonement. We shall see that the definition of God's justice implied behind the popular view of atonement diverges from Paul's. This is so because this popular view limits the notion of justice to human law court experience of justice, whereas Paul and the biblical imagery is richer.

The concept of justice is indeed a legal term and that must be included in the biblical concept as well. We frequently define justice as "conformity to a norm," or as "giving what is due according to legal requirement." However, when we limit the concept of justice to this strict legal definition, we miss much of what Paul and all of the Bible add. In strict legality and based on our experience of human judges, we say that ideally "justice is blind." Judges mete out their judgments with neutrality, based solely on the merits of a case. When the popular theory of atonement applies that concept to God, then God's justice is conceived as that impartial activity of God rewarding and punishing according to our due.

Paul's concept of God's justice is not totally devoid of forensic or legal traits. There is certainly some sense that God acts ac-

19

cording to proper standard, and there is also some sense that God calls people to account for their behavior. But these same words which function as legal terms also appear in contexts where they convey, not neutrality on God's part, but active involvement and saving activity. While God acts according to proper standard, it is not to a human standard, but divine. While God calls people to account, God does not passively condemn them but seeks to rescue them from condemnation, to help them to measure up to what they should be. When Paul speaks of God's justice, it is never defined as God's wrath (which is a separate concept, as we shall see), and it is never defined as vindictive punishment for sin. Rather, it is a saving justice. In this usage Paul takes over Jewish and Christian traditions before him. We will better understand Paul if we look briefly at those earlier traditions.

Jewish Background

In the Old Testament, the Hebrew word which underlies Paul's Greek word for justice (*dikaiosynē*) is *tsedaqah,* and there are also adjectival and verbal forms of these words.[1] When applied to God, they sometimes retain their legal meaning, but they also often denote fidelity to the demands of a relationship, specifically the relationship of covenant. A cursory view of Old Testament texts reveals this meaning of God's justice.[2] Since the demands of covenant were so varied, God's justice was associated with many varied functions, but all of them saving activity: mercy, triumph, faithfulness, defense, steadfast love, law, etc. God establishes covenant and thereby establishes the criteria of fidelity to covenant that becomes the very essence of biblical justice: "Thou art the Lord, the God who didst choose Abram . . . and didst make with

---

[1] It might be helpful to observe here that the English translations of the Bible use two different words to translate either the Greek or the Hebrew: "righteousness" and "justice." The former is of Anglo-Saxon root and the latter is of Latin. While they may have different nuances, the nuances are not sustained and English translations vary as to which word should be used in a particular text. We will use the terms interchangeably, trying to understand their meaning from their biblical contexts.

[2] See Elizabeth R. Achtemeier, "Righteousness in the Old Testament," in George A. Buttrick, ed., *The Interpreter's Dictionary of the Bible* (Nashville: Abingdon Press, 1962), 4:80–85.

him the covenant . . . and thou hast fulfilled thy promise, for thou art righteous" (Neh 9:7-8). What God establishes God sustains and defends: "The steadfast love of the Lord is from everlasting to everlasting upon those who fear him, and his righteousness to children's children" (Ps 103:17). "I will save my people . . . and they shall be my people and I will be their God, in faithfulness and righteousness" (Zech 8:7-8).

Even without explicit mention of covenant it is interesting to see how many texts relate God's justice to salvation, which was, of course, the principal purpose of the covenant established through Moses: "I bring near my deliverance [*tsedaqah*], it is not far off, and my salvation will not tarry" (Isa 46:13); "In his day Judah will be saved, and Israel will dwell securely. And this is the name by which he will be called: 'The Lord is our righteousness' " (Jer 23:6); "I have not hid thy saving help [*tsedaqah*] within my heart, I have spoken of thy faithfulness and thy salvation" (Ps 40:10). In view of these assertions, it is clear that those texts which speak of God's justice in a forensic sense of rewarding or punishing need to be amplified by this truth of God's saving action.

Sometimes even in the forensic use of *tsedaqah* the word is reserved for the saving activity as opposed to the punishing. In Psalm 69:27 the psalmist prays that the wicked have punishment upon punishment, and "no access to [God's] righteousness."[3] In Daniel 9:4-18, God's justice, far from being equated with punishing wrath, is expressly contrasted with it. Sometimes one has the sense that the punishment of the wicked is not so much God's active decision as God's allowing sin to reap its own consequences. "If a man does not repent, . . . he falls into the hole which he has made" (Ps 7:12, 15); "The wicked are snared in the work of their own hands" (Ps 9:16). Mostly, the punishing is of Israel's enemies, "all the nations that forget God" (Ps 9:17), and so put themselves outside of God's saving offer. *Tsedaqah* is not used of God's punishing action toward the chosen people. Even when they are unfaithful, God reaches out in faithfulness to restore the

---

[3]This Jerusalem Bible translation captures the use of *tsedaqah* more clearly than the RSV, which we have been using.

relationship and to bring Israel to salvation: "In thy faithfulness answer me, in thy righteousness! . . . In thy righteousness bring me out of trouble!" (Ps 143:1, 11); "Destruction is decreed overflowing with righteousness" (Isa 10:22).

If we do perceive a forensic dimension to God's justice, we must also say that it is not as a neutral judge meting out what people are due, but rather as one who upholds the right and who defends the victims of injustice. If God is indeed aware of right and wrong according to divine law and brings all to judgment, it is not without a faithful and constant offer to bring the unjust back into justice once again. God's justice is not divorced from God's mercy. Both justice and mercy are two complementary ways of describing God's saving activity. In fact, it is interesting to note that sometimes the Greek Septuagint translation of the Hebrew Old Testament uses "mercy" (*eleos*) to render *tsedaqah,* as it also uses "justice" (*dikaiosynē*) to render "steadfast covenant love" (*hesed*). Second Isaiah puts God's justice explicitly in its forensic or law-court setting, but shows it to be a relational activity, a justice which saves: "Declare and present your case. . . . There is no other god besides me, a righteous God and a Savior. . . . Only in the Lord . . . are righteousness and strength. . . . In the Lord all the offspring of Israel shall triumph and glory" (Isa 45:21, 24-25).

Second Isaiah offers us occasion to perceive another important dimension of God's justice, i.e., that it reaches out especially to the poor and the oppressed, to those on the margins of society, to those most in need of justice. In chapter 58:1-9, the prophet describes Israel in its sinfulness calling out as if it were righteous and asking for God's righteous (saving) judgments. God replies that God will be near and Israel will experience God's justice if it shares bread with the hungry, shelter with the homeless, and clothing with the naked. God's saving justice is experienced not just as personal salvation, but as effective within society and in the situations of people who feel the effects of injustice in the political and social structures of their world. The prophet thus echoes the longstanding tradition of Israel concerning God's justice as reaching out to the oppressed: "The Lord God executes justice for the fatherless and the widow, and loves the sojourner, giving him food and clothing" (Deut 10:18); "God executes justice for the oppressed, gives food to the hungry" (Ps 146:7).

The new note that Second Isaiah adds to the concept of God's justice is its strong eschatological dimension. This is a theme picked up also by apocalyptic literature and the literature of Judaism as it moves into the time of Jesus. With an increasing emphasis on human sinfulness and injustice there comes an increasing emphasis on hope in a God who will ultimately exercise justice as a saving justice in the future: "I bring near my deliverance [saving justice], it is not far off, and my salvation will not tarry" (Isa 46:13); "In this, O Lord, thy righteousness and goodness will be declared, when thou art merciful to those who have no store of good works" (2 Esdr 8:36). Within this eschatological expectation there is also room to render account of human suffering and the struggle to know why God is taking so long to achieve this work of justice. Human suffering is seen as somehow salvific, and the just who suffer expect that God will ultimately vindicate them: "The righteous live forever, and their reward is with the Lord; the Most High takes care of them. . . . He will put on righteousness as a breastplate, and wear impartial justice as a helmet" (Wis 5:15, 18).

Finally, in the background of Paul, the Dead Sea Scrolls of the Qumran community gather the varied elements of Jewish tradition and carry them forward with the new phrase that will become so important for Paul, "the righteousness of God" (*dikaiosynē theou*). The Qumran authors keep the forensic nature of God's justice while also understanding it as God's saving action in fidelity to covenant.

The Justice of God in Paul

The above selection of Old Testament texts showing God's justice as fidelity to covenant provides the base for understanding Paul's vision of the justice of God as saving activity. Paul, of course, does not begin Christianity. He is influenced by the way the Old Testament is reinterpreted by early Christian tradition before him. Thus, the concept of God's justice seems to have pre-Pauline roots in the early Church as well as in the Old Testament. These early teachings would, of course, have made the new point, beyond their Jewish heritage, that God's justice is now manifest specifically in Christ. Some, for instance, see in the style of Paul's 1 Corinthians 1:30 an indication of an early Church formula naming now the crucified and risen Christ as the manifestation of God's saving justice. Paul adds the formula to the summation of his previous discussion of Christ as God's wisdom. As Christ has become for us God's wisdom, so he becomes "for us righteousness, sanctification and redemption from God." Likewise, Romans 3:25, with its contorted multiplication of phrases and some non-Pauline vocabulary, may contain early Christian confessions showing Christ as God's righteousness: "God put forward Jesus as an expiation by his blood to show God's righteousness, because in his divine forbearance he had passed over former sins."

Paul will develop further the concept of Christ showing God's righteousness, linking it more closely with what that righteousness achieves in us, showing its universal dimensions, and stressing that it comes through faith and not the law. We will consider in a later chapter the effects of God's justice on humanity, i.e., righteousness on the human side. For now, we wish to illustrate Paul's teaching about God's justice as God's saving activity manifest in Christ. For this we concentrate on the passages that speak explicitly about "the righteousness of God" (*dikaiosynē theou*). Discussion on this very phrase, "the righteousness of God," highlights the divine and human dimensions of justice.

There has been a great deal of controversy over this phrase, especially because of Catholic-Protestant polemic over the centuries. In our ecumenical age there has been an easing of polemics and growing enlightenment over the phrase. We follow the suggestions of the person who has been the most influential in our generation for moving past the controversy, Ernst Käsemann.[4] Debate has been over whether *dikaiosynē theou* is an objective genitive or a subjective one, i.e., whether the righteousness refers to what is possessed by human beings as offered by God or to

[4]Ernst Käsemann, *New Testament Questions of Today* (Philadelphia: Fortress Press, 1969) 168–182.

what is possessed by God as God's own. Käsemann suggests that the phrase should refer to both meanings, since it contains the idea of justice as both power and gift. Justice is surely God's action (power), but it genuinely effects something in human beings (gift).

In any case, we concentrate now on the subjective genitive, on justice as God's possession. We see it especially as God's activity, not just personal virtue, and as saving activity, not just as impartial law-court sentencing. Three passages using the phrase will highlight this meaning.

> [16]I am not ashamed of the gospel: it is the power of God for salvation to everyone who has faith, to the Jew first and also to the Greek. [17]For in it the righteousness of God is revealed through faith for faith; as it is written, "He who through faith is righteous shall live" (Rom 1:16-17).

These verses, in effect, provide the topic sentences of Paul's Letter to the Romans in which much of what we are calling a theology of atonement in the broad sense is contained. We see first of all that Paul finds God's justice manifest in what Christ does for us. In this passage he refers to Christ as "the gospel." For Paul the "good news" is not simply teaching or preaching about Jesus, much less the written works of gospels which did not yet exist, but the communication of the risen Christ himself. In the preceding verses 1-6, Paul says he is set apart for the gospel concerning Jesus who is incarnate and risen "in power," so that all might ultimately belong to him. Now, in this Christ who is "good news" Paul sees manifest God's justice as activity and as saving activity, as he forms a parallel between the revelation of righteousness in verse 17 and the power of God for salvation in verse 16.

When Paul says that the gospel is "for everyone who has faith," he expresses God's justice as universal in scope, as open to all. This is confirmed by Paul's adding "to the Jew first and also to the Greek." This becomes one of Paul's central concerns about God's saving justice, its reaching even to the Gentiles. God may have reached out in a special way to Israel, as the words "to the

Jew first" would indicate, but ultimately God's justice is universal in scope, "also to the Greek." Finally, there may be in the quotation from Habakkuk some hints of God's fidelity to covenant as the foundation of God's righteousness. In the original Hebrew text (Hab 2:4) it reads, "The righteous shall live by *his* faith" and implies a position of faithfulness on the part of the believer. In the Septuagint it reads, "The righteous shall live by my faithfulness," implying God's act of fidelity to covenant. Paul does not use either pronoun, and certainly deepens the meaning of the text to embrace his notion of justification by faith. It may be, however, that in leaving the ambiguity of pronouns, Paul implies not only the human response of faith but God's fidelity to covenant now understood as the covenant established in Christ.

This indication that God's justice means God's fidelity to covenant receives special emphasis in Romans 3:1-5:

> ¹Then what advantage has the Jew? Or what is the value of circumcision? ²Much in every way. To begin with, the Jews are entrusted with the oracles of God. ³What if some were unfaithful? Does their faithlessness nullify the faithfulness of God? ⁴By no means! Let God be true though every man be false, as it is written,
>
> > "That thou mayest be justified in thy words,
> > and prevail when thou art judged."
>
> ⁵But if our wickedness serves to show the justice of God, what shall we say?

The context of this passage is the discussion of human sinfulness in which Paul has indicted the Jews as well as the Gentiles for rebellion against God. (We will give full consideration to sin and its consequences in the following chapter.) Paul anticipates questions that this will raise, and this first section of chapter 3 addresses such questions. In what is known as a diatribe, Paul posits a fictitious opponent who raises the objections to his teaching so that Paul might then offer his refutations. In the verses that we are considering the first objection is met: If Israel itself is to be condemned for its sinfulness, then what is the point of the revelation that God gave it? Either God gave false testimony or God is unfaithful to Israel.

The question Paul posits is no secondary matter, but is rather crucial to understanding the entire action of God in salvation history. Paul answers that circumcision is still of value if one can distinguish circumcision as sign of promise from circumcision as law. God did not give false witness to Israel; Israel is in fact the bearer of God's oracles, i.e., his self-revelation, his promises, his work of salvation. These promises had validity. Nevertheless, promise still leaves room for response and, in fact, calls for it. Thus, while God's promise is sincere, there is possibility of rebellion, ignorance, sin, or complacency on the human side. While Israel's circumcision held value as promise, its value as law was compromised because Israel did not keep the law. It fell into sin as readily as the Gentiles without the law. If this is the case, however, then the question arises of whether the promises still remain; is God faithful to Israel? Paul gives a resounding yes to this question and thus brings the topic of God's fidelity to covenant (understood here as God's oracles) to center stage in this passage. He thus anticipates what he will detail in Romans 9–11 about how God remains faithful to Israel while opening salvation to the Gentiles.

Because of the way in which the topic is framed, Paul also picks up another thread that we saw in the apocalyptic setting of Judaism, namely, the sharp contrast between God's fidelity and human infidelity or sinfulness. God's faithfulness to covenant is not patterned on human faithfulness. On the contrary, God's fidelity is equated with God's being "true," i.e., firm and reliable, while human beings are characterized as "false," i.e., not measuring up, standing on privilege, self-justifying, lacking responsibility. There seem to be some further eschatological indications in that Paul sees an ongoing display of God's fidelity. Literally, he says, "Let God *become* true," as if the divine work were a continuing conquest, an overcoming of human faithlessness in a salvation history moving toward culmination in the end time.

Paul seems at this point to be moving beyond consideration of Israel alone to a universal description, since "all" are described as false. Finally, this universal description is put into a forensic setting by the quotation from Psalm 51:4. The psalm develops the same contrast which we have been describing in this text of Romans. In verse 3, prior to our citation, the psalmist had acknowledged his sinfulness ("My sin is ever before me"). Then, in the verse Paul quotes, he said that it serves to highlight only that much more God's justice as it seeks to eliminate sin ("So that thou art justified in thy sentence and blameless in thy judgment"). Paul not only keeps the contrast, but takes over the Septuagint translation which modifies the Hebrew. In our text it accentuates the quality of God's justice as fidelity to covenant. Instead of humanity's being judged, God is put to trial and is vindicated: "[Let God be true or faithful] that thou mayest be justified in thy words [i.e., stressing the promises rather than the sentencing] and prevail when thou art judged [stressing God's being judged rather than his judging]."

Up to this point we have not yet encountered Paul's phrase "the righteousness of God." That appears in verse 5, where Paul introduces a new objection to be treated in the subsequent verses. It is the question of whether God is unjust in punishing sin if God is supposed to be a faithful God. That objection in another diatribe follows from the one we have been considering about the value of Judaism. We are not concerned with the next objection, but with how Paul hooks it up with the prior discussion. Paul says, in effect, "If all that we have said in these first verses of chapter 3 are true, then what shall we say about the next objection?" The interesting point for our purposes is that when Paul sums up all that he has said in the first verses of chapter 3, he asserts, "If our wickedness [injustice] serves to show the justice of God. . . ." Thus, for Paul, God's justice, while it has forensic overtones, also stresses God's fidelity to covenant. It is in sharp contrast to and in spite of human infidelity and sin, with universal outreach, in an eschatological or apocalyptic setting. At heart, God's justice is God's saving activity in a world which sorely needs it.

What we have been saying about Christ as manifestation of God's justice as a saving activity is expressed most explicitly in what many consider the heart of the doctrinal teaching of Romans, in 3:21-26. We cite the pertinent verses:

[21]The righteousness of God has been manifested apart from the law, although the law and the prophets bear witness to it, [22]the righteousness of God through faith in Jesus Christ for all who believe. For there is no distinction; [23]since all have sinned and fall short of the glory of God, [24]they are justified by his grace as a gift, through the redemption which is in Christ Jesus, [25a]whom God put forward as an expiation by his blood, to be received by faith. [b]This was to show God's righteousness, because in his divine forbearance he had passed over former sins; [26]it was to prove at the present time that he himself is righteous and that he justifies him who has faith in Jesus.

This passage follows closely upon the previous one that we have just analyzed, so that in many ways it carries over the meaning of God's justice as presented in the earlier text. But now in this later passage Paul moves to a more explicit treatment of the theme. He has just finished the first section of his letter dealing with human sinfulness among both Jews and Gentiles. He has indicated in that section that this should not nullify God's justice. Now he begins the positive statement of his letter, that God's justice manifests itself in the face of human sinfulness.

The beginning verses highlight the theology that Paul stresses regarding the "justice of God," namely that it is apart from law through faith. The central verses, 24-25a, highlight the means by which atonement is achieved by Christ as the manifestation of God's justice. We will examine these points later on. For now our concern is to give one final example from Paul about the basic meaning of God's justice as a subjective genitive. Paul says it is the same meaning as that of the Old Testament, since the Law and the Prophets as Scripture bear witness to it, although now it is manifest specifically in Christ. That means that God is actively engaged in doing something about human sin and infidelity, not ultimately to punish or to dissolve covenant, but to recreate it. Paul shows again how this is in sharp contrast to human beings, "since all have sinned" and that it is a justice universal in scope, since "there is no distinction."

Without going into detail on how Christ shows God's justice in verses 24-25a, we can at least point out that the work of justice somehow involves the suffering of Christ, reminiscent of the Old Testament insight that God's justice will in some way render human suffering salvific and that God's justice will ultimately bring the vindication of the just who suffer (cf. Wis 5; Isa 53). The cross of Christ also intimates that God's justice does not take lightly human sinfulness or simply overlook it. While God does not exercise vindictive justice, God does do something that corrects the injustices in humanity. What is intimated in the verses about the cross is made explicit in verse 25b, when Paul says that God's justice is shown in Christ because divine forbearance has been exercised toward sins of the past. In other words, in the Old Testament, God in divine justice, wanting more than to punish sin, looked forward to the eschatological time in which God would provide the means of ultimate atonement. But God could not exercise tolerance forever without making the situation right. That time has now arrived in Christ, so that God's justice can be fully exercised in bringing humanity out of its sin and injustice. Thus, God's justice, while it has a forensic quality of holding people accountable, is also an activity and a saving justice.

In the last verse of our passage Paul states explicitly his view of God's justice as we have been defining it. He takes what seem in the previous verses to be traditional formulae about Christ's sacrificial work of redemption and adds to them the explanation that these show God's justice not to be purely forensic justice, impartial rewarding or punishing, or simple conformity to norms, but rather God's positive activity whereby God acts to make us just. Commentators will point out that even the phrase "he himself is righteous" is not to be understood simply as God's inner virtue or attribute, but rather God's movement toward us, God's fidelity to covenant and activity to make us just in spite of our sins.[5] Such a justice of God reveals God in action, which culminates in what Paul says in his last comment, "he justifies him who has faith in Jesus," i.e., God is just in the very act of justifying. Finally, for Paul all of this takes place in an apocalyptic con-

---

[5] See Brendan Byrne, S.J., *Reckoning with Romans: A Contemporary Reading of Paul's Gospel* (Wilmington, Del.: Michael Glazier, 1986) 86: "He is 'righteous,' faithful, precisely in his justifying act, creatively restoring believers to full relationship."

text as the beginning of the new age, as present eschatology in which God begins the final victory not only over the hearts of individuals but over all of creation itself. This is clear from Paul's opening remark in this text that God's righteousness has *now* been manifest. "Now" is to be understood in a temporal sense and not just as a word indicating logical sequence. Even more clearly, Paul states at the end of this text that God's justice is proven "in the present time," the final eschatological era already begun.

The Wrath of God

[18]The wrath of God is revealed from heaven against all ungodliness and wickedness of men. . . .
[24]Therefore God gave them up in the lusts of their hearts (Rom 1:18, 24).

What we have been saying about God's justice may also be confirmed by consideration of a seeming contrast, the theme of the wrath of God. If God's justice is divine fidelity to covenant and God's saving action, why would Paul use a phrase like "the wrath of God"? Does the phrase disprove what we have been saying? The answer is no, but this requires a brief consideration of Paul's meaning for "the wrath of God." Paul's use of the phrase derives from his Old Testament background and not from Greek culture. Hence, it does not imply capricious activity on God's part or vindictive emotion within God, as the phrase might suggest to us in English. Some biblical scholars go so far as to dissociate the phrase from any reference to a movement within God, and to relate it to God's activity toward the world or even to impersonal automatic consequences of sin somewhat distanced from God altogether.[6]

There are good reasons for seeing God's wrath as God's effective activity rather than affective quality. The phrase may be the remnant of a primitive religious consciousness which began as fear of the transcendent but which became more and more reasoned

---

[6]For a discussion of varied viewpoints, see D. E. H. Whiteley, *The Theology of St. Paul* (Philadelphia: Fortress Press, 1972) 61–72.

as the incompatibility of God with sin. Primitive religion has a sense of awe in the face of divine mystery. The negative side of this awe is a fear of what one cannot explain and a projection into the divine of anger and caprice. Israelite religion may have inherited this primitive religious instinct but transformed it into a consciousness compatible with Hebrew belief in the mercy and covenant fidelity of Yahweh. The Old Testament contains hints of a vindictive or emotionally angry God in some ancient traditions like Exodus 4:24: "At a lodging place on the way the Lord met him [Moses] and sought to kill him." Almost all biblical scholars recognize, however, that the Old Testament evolves, putting less emphasis on emotion in God and more on the consequences of sin and God's need to eradicate injustice.

More frequently in later Old Testament writing "wrath" is used without the phrase "of God," as if it were an objective or impersonal force dealing with sin and not a personal involvement of God at all. Thus, Zephaniah 1:14-15 says, "The great day of the Lord is near. . . . A day of wrath is that day, a day of distress and anguish, a day of ruin and devastation." Paul seems to pick up this latter pattern, speaking of wrath as an objective force without using "of God." A good example is found in 1 Thessalonians 1:10: ". . . Jesus who delivers us from the wrath to come." (See also 1 Thess 5:9; Rom 2:5, 8; 5:9.) In Romans 2:8-9, Paul explains that "wrath and fury" are really "tribulation and distress for every human being." Wrath is not described as emotion in God.

While these texts are strong evidence that the wrath of God should not indicate God's anger or hatred of sinners, they leave more debate over whether one can divorce the concept completely from God's personal involvement. After all, even those passages which speak only of "the wrath" can still imply that it is God's wrath. In fact, the passage which we cited from Zephaniah 1:14-15 continues in verse 18 to speak of "the day of the wrath of the Lord," and Paul's reference in Romans 2:8-9 is in a section that speaks of the wrath as "God's" in 1:18. It does seem clear, however, that this wrath, even when it entails God's personal involvement, does not entail vindictive anger, but God's activity. Even those who hold strongly for wrath as description of God's affectivity make equally strong claims that God's wrath is not the same as human wrath and is not the desire to destroy sinners.[7]

We may best conclude that the phrase "wrath of God" depicts the mirror image of God's justice. It is the negative side of God's saving action. Since God's fidelity to covenant demands human response and responsibility, wrath is what one experiences when one rejects God's offer of justice. God does not change in any way the divine behavior toward us, but because we close ourselves off from it, we experience that behavior as our self-condemnation rather than as salvation. While "wrath of God" is very personal and even emotion-laden terminology, its purpose is to highlight the absolute incompatibility of God with sin, to take seriously the reality of sin, and to show that God must do something about sin if God is to exercise true justice. God's saving activity cannot simply overlook sin. If human freedom resolutely persists in sin, then human freedom must also be responsible for the consequences of that rejection. In Romans 1:18ff., Paul sums up this reality, showing "wrath" as the consequences of human sinfulness while not necessarily divorcing wrath completely from God's personal involvement. Three times in that chapter (vv. 24, 26, 28) Paul says, "God gave them up," i.e., God allowed sin to work its course and to bring its own condemnation. When free human beings among both Jews and Greeks refused fidelity to relationship with God, then all relationships broke down and human degradation and alienation followed as consequence. God respects human freedom and allows sin to bring its own punishment.

One further indication of how far God's wrath is removed from a notion of vindictive anger is found in the consistent biblical teaching that even God's wrath is in service of God's justice. God allows sin to work its course only so that human beings in their freedom will abandon sin and open themselves to God's saving justice. Hosea 11:8-9 highlights this from the Old Testament: "How can I give you up, O Ephraim! . . . I will not execute my fierce anger . . . for I am God and not man." Paul continues this same theme. In 1 Thessalonians 5:9, he insists, "God has not

[7]C. E. B. Cranfield, *Romans: A Shorter Commentary* (Grand Rapids: William B. Eerdmans Publishing Co., 1985) 28–29.

destined us for wrath, but to obtain salvation through our Lord Jesus Christ." In Romans 9:22-23, he says that God has shown wrath in order to show power; has allowed "vessels of wrath," i.e., has allowed Israel to experience the consequences of its sins in order to make known "vessels of mercy," i.e., in order to draw the good effect of opening salvation also to the Gentiles. If Romans 11 is further commentary on Romans 9, then the wrath of God toward Israel is for the ultimate salvation even of Israel itself: "God has consigned all men to disobedience, that he may have mercy upon all" (Rom 11:32).

Thus, both the justice of God and the wrath of God are not so much attributes of God as they are terms that describe God's activity. They are both "revealed" (Rom 1:17-18) and are indeed two sides of the same coin. The wrath of God is revealed as correlative to God's saving power, as a necessary effect of God's justice in a free but sinful world. Finally, for Paul, God's wrath, like God's justice, is an eschatological reality which will achieve its full consequences in the future, although we begin to experience it partially in the present consequences of sin. (cf. 1 Thess 1:10 [future wrath] with 2:16 [wrath beginning in the present], and Rom 2:9 and 5:9 [future reality] with 1:18 and 3:5 [present anticipation of the wrath].) As apocalyptic realities, both wrath of God and justice of God embrace a social dimension, that is, they represent God's activity not just toward individuals and for personal salvation but toward a world that needs to be rescued from the power of evil and toward a creation that yearns for final transformation.

2

The Need of Atonement

Having established in Paul that God's justice is God's saving activity, we can then proceed to consider how God exercises that justice, part of what we are calling "Paul's theology of atonement" in the broad sense of that term. We will, however, obtain a clearer picture of the process of atonement if we first sharpen our picture of why we need the atonement in the first place. Just what does God see when God looks at the human race? Just how bad is human unfaithfulness in contrast with God's fidelity to covenant? These questions lead us in this chapter to describe Paul's vision of the human race without Christ, a world enslaved to sin and all its related powers, a world in radical need of atonement. The picture is not a happy one, but Paul thinks it is a realistic one. Paul's depiction of a world trapped in sin is not to make pessimists of us all but to set the stage for a greater appreciation of how much God does for us in Christ's work of atonement.

Paul's overriding description of humanity without Christ is of humanity enslaved to sin. In considering Paul's theology of sin, two aspects are significant for our purposes: first, that sin is best conceived as a state or condition, a stance or an attitude, rather than simply one or a series of discrete actions; second, that sin has serious social dimensions related to the situation of social injustice and oppression that Christ must overcome in his work of atonement. We will highlight these aspects of sin by a brief analysis of the pertinent key words in Paul. Notice that the conditions which we incorporate into our one term "sin" are expressed by several terms in Paul.

Sin as Ungodliness and Injustice

The wrath of God is revealed from heaven against all *ungodli-ness [asebeia] and wickedness [adikia]* of men who by their *wickedness* suppress the truth (Rom 1:18, italics added).

The predominant vocabulary of sin in the section of Romans 1:18-32 is that of "ungodliness" (*asebeia*) and "wickedness" (*adikia*). Sin is first of all ungodliness or godlessness, i.e., a basic stance which rejects God and God's designs for creation. It is a question of willful disregard, as Paul describes in the following verses. There the Gentiles, who could know God from human reason or experience, are said to have refused the "honor" due God and the "thanks" which God deserves (vv. 19-21). Paul is not so much concerned with theory or intellectual debate about natural knowledge of God as with the active engagement of the human person in his or her relationship with God. Our very existence as creatures becomes occasion for the experience of a transcendent reality. "Creatureliness" bespeaks a Creator. But intellect is part of a total person who must turn toward the Creator with choice and feeling. In refusing to accept God as source of all that one is and does, in refusing to thank God, one sets not only intellect but one's entire person against God. Paul summarizes in verse 21 the condition of the Gentiles who lack honor and thanks as having their "senseless minds darkened." Literally, this phrase reads, "their uncomprehending hearts were darkened." "Heart" depicts the person as willing and feeling as well as thinking. We are talking about a total stance or position turned away from God.

To understand this situation in contemporary terms, we might say that in turning away from God one ultimately turns away from all that gives meaning to human existence. One seeks to make some penultimate reality the ground or source of meaning. One refuses to accept the condition of being creature and substitutes oneself or some other creature for the Creator. In verse 23 Paul says that darkened hearts end up "exchanging the glory of the immortal God for images resembling mortal man or birds or animals or reptiles." In effect, for Paul, godlessness or ungodliness is not simply rejection of God but also idolatry, the setting up of someone or something else as ultimate object of honor and thanks. To speak again in contemporary language, there is for Paul no such thing as a true atheist. Behind theoretical atheism lies the existential fact of either acknowledging the true ground of reality, whatever one calls it, or esteeming a created reality as ultimate, setting up a false god and distorting the meaning of human existence.

If rejection of God is the elevating of false gods and the suppression of what gives ultimate meaning to human life, then we may accurately say that it is the suppression of the truth and the acceptance of a lie. Paul says both (vv. 18 and 25). This again is not simply theoretical or speculative error but deliberate choice with ethical implications. Paul says that the lie is in worship and service of the creature rather than the Creator (v. 25). This is the core of sin, then, a state or an attitude underlying all eventual activity.

To highlight this dimension of sin and to show that it is primarily a state or an attitude is not to limit sin to intention or to a purely private sphere. Indeed, sin shows itself in action, and an essential element of sin is its destruction of social relations. When, in Romans 1:18, Paul speaks of God's wrath against "ungodliness," he says it is also against "wickedness" or "injustice" (*adikia*). In fact, as he continues the verse he speaks only of injustice which "suppresses the truth," as if the full reality of sin can be summed up in injustice. In exploring the general meaning of *adikia,* one could accurately define it as the opposite of *dikaiosynē,* "justice" (cf. Rom 6:13). We have yet to consider fully the meaning of justice in human beings, but we have seen how justice takes its definition first of all from God's justice. Now if God's justice is primarily his fidelity to relationship, then injustice in humanity would be that lack of fidelity. Because of this general meaning, *adikia* is sometimes translated simply as "wickedness." In Romans 3:5 and 9:14, this meaning of *adikia* as infidelity to relationship is explicit. Romans 3:5, as we have seen, contrasts our infidelity with God's fidelity. In Romans 9:14, Paul asks whether God's activity toward Israel shows injustice on God's part, meaning infidelity to covenant.

Notwithstanding this general meaning of *adikia,* we may also find more specific social dimensions. In the same way that God's justice is concerned especially with the outsider, with the poor and with those on the margins of society, so human injustice is the breakdown of relations experienced primarily in their social ramifications. Paul does say this, though he does not express the thought the way we would with contemporary language of oppression. In Romans 1:24-31, he shows where the rejection of God and suppression of the truth lead. God's "wrath" lets sin work its course. In these three sections where Paul says "God gave them up," the consequences of human sinfulness are described as social in nature. In the first two sections the effects are seen in sexual disorder, itself a breakdown of social relations, whereby human sexuality becomes a means of oppression. Some persons are no longer ends to be respected for themselves, but means or objects for another's pleasure. In the third section, where Paul uses *adikia* (wickedness) explicitly, it is paralleled with a list of vices that show predominantly social injustices that follow upon the breakdown of human relations: "envy, murder, strife, deceit, malignity"; being "slanderers, haters of God, insolent, haughty, boastful, inventors of evil, disobedient to parents, foolish, faithless, heartless, ruthless" (vv. 29-31).

Thus, especially in Romans 1:18-32, Paul gives us the words ungodliness (*asebeia*) and injustice (*adikia*) to describe what we call sin, above all as a stance against God that entails distorted and broken social relations as well. We may generally divide this part of chapter 1 of Romans into two halves in which the first (vv. 18-23) develops the description of *asebeia* and the second (vv. 24-32) develops the theme of *adikia,* as we have shown above. Most commentators, however, would not separate the sections as if *asebeia* concerned one kind of sin and *adikia* another. We have already indicated that 1:18 concludes by having *asebeia* absorbed into *adikia* so that the latter represents the total human disposition which suppresses the truth. We may, therefore, join the two halves of Romans 1:18-32, interpreting Paul to mean that rejection of God is manifest in social injustice. Given our present-day concerns with social injustice, we may carry the analysis farther. Could Paul not imply that in point of fact, social oppression and social sin are at the heart of human disorder and that our very concept of God is distorted in order to justify and to condone this sin? Religion becomes another ideological tool to justify activity that really oppresses and dehumanizes. *Adikia* suppresses the truth that results in idolatry to reinforce that very injustice (1:18).[1]

Sin as Missing the Target

> [12]Let not sin [*hamartia*] therefore reign in your mortal bodies, to make you obey their passions. [13]Do not yield your members to sin [*hamartia*] as instruments of wickedness (Rom 6:12-13).

The definition of sin as stance or attitude and the relation of sin to social injustice is clearly presented by another word that Paul uses, *hamartia*. In its etymological sense the word means "missing the target," implying that sin is failure to be what one should be.[2] To more fully elaborate, humanity is to reflect God's glory, i.e., to reflect God's own life as it is revealed to us. Sin is failure to do this. In Romans 3:23, Paul says explicitly that all have sinned and "fall short of the glory of God." Now this failure to be in harmony with what God is, is certainly manifest in actions, but the actions flow from a basic stance or attitude. Paul conveys this point by using most often the word *hamartia* when he is speaking of what we call sin, and by using it in the singular. Almost always when Paul speaks of "sins" in the plural these texts are explicit or implicit citations from the Old Testament, e.g., Romans 4:7; 11:27; and 1 Thessalonians 2:16 (cf. Gen 15:16), or they are references to previously existing liturgical formulae, e.g., "Christ died for our sins" (1 Cor 15:3; Gal 1:4). Otherwise, Paul refers to "sin" in the singular. While one or another text (e.g., 2 Cor 11:7) may use "sin" to refer to an action, the overwhelming meaning is that of a power or force that underlies all

---

[1]Juan Luis Segundo, *The Humanist Christology of Paul*, vol. 3 of *Jesus of Nazareth Yesterday and Today* (Maryknoll, N.Y.: Orbis Books, 1986) 13-27.

[2]Paul likewise uses another term, *paraptoma* (trespass) to describe what we call sin (cf. Rom 5:15-20). This imagery of "misstepping" is not far from the imagery of "missing the target," so that *paraptoma* is virtually synonymous with *hamartia*. We will not, therefore, treat the former word separately.

actions, the state of the sinner before God. The appearance of "sin" in this sense predominates in Romans 5-8, where it is used over thirty times.

Not only does Paul use "sin" in the singular in this section, but he also personifies it. Sin comes alive as a character that enters us, controls us, and thereby leads us to all manner of rebellion. In Romans we have, as it were, a kind of morality play in which the character "Everyone" becomes the victim of the villain "Sin." "Sin came into the world through one man" (5:12), and "Sin reigned" (5:21). This reign of Sin is not merely external to humanity but exerts its power internally: "Our sinful passions were at work in our members" (7:5); "Sin dwells within me" (7:20). This power takes full possession and control: "If you yield yourselves to any one as obedient slaves, you are slaves of the one whom you obey. . . . You were once slaves of sin" (6:16-17). The power and dominion of Sin do not necessarily lead to continuous acts of rebellion or desire. Sin may be dormant, but the person is not free from its control: "I was once alive apart from the law, but when the commandment came, sin revived and I died" (7:9). So pervasive is the reign of Sin and so persistent its presence that eventually it crushes Everyone left to the powers of his or her own resources: "Sin deceived me and . . . killed me" (7:11). Thus, *hamartia* reflects in Paul the state of mind or attitude of the person that precedes any individual sinful acts.

Once again, however, for this word as for the previous ones which we considered, Paul does not imply that sin is essentially private. From his thought we can extract what we would today call a solidarity in sin, a communal dimension such that every sin affects society around us and the entire human race. This sense of solidarity in sin is derived from what Paul attributes to the sin of Adam and what theology calls "original" sin. The pertinent passage is Romans 5:12-21, especially its first statement in verse 12: [12a]"Therefore as sin came into the world through one man [b]and death through sin, [c]and so death spread to all men [d]because all men sinned." The thrust of verses 12-21 is to show our solidarity in Christ for reconciliation, something that we will treat when we consider Christ's work of atonement. In explaining solidarity in Christ, however, Paul does so by contrasting it with the solidarity of humanity in its sinfulness. This leads him to speak of the role of Adam. While the Old Testament had some teaching on human solidarity in Adam, Paul has even more profound insight because of what he knows about solidarity in Christ. We might say that the hindsight of revelation about life in Christ sheds further light even on human collusion in sin.

Thus, Paul speaks about the causality that Adam initiates regarding our sins. This causality is described especially in verses 12c-d, 13, 14 and makes more explicit what is contained in the Jewish traditions. In Genesis, the sin of Adam is described in order to show sin as human responsibility and not God's work, but there is not much emphasis on Adam's causing succeeding sin. Later Jewish tradition rereads Genesis, affirming more of a link between Adam and his posterity: "O Adam, what have you done! For though it was you who sinned, the fall was not yours alone but ours also who are your descendants" (4 Ezra 7:118). Still, this claim leaves questions. Is Adam responsible simply because he sets bad example? Or is Adam so responsible for our fall that we bear no responsibility ourselves? Judaism itself battled over this latter question. 2 Baruch 54:15-19 affirmed, "Adam is, therefore, not the cause, save only of his own soul, but each one of us has been the Adam of his own soul." Paul takes up the Genesis story once again and finds the middle ground: Adam is indeed not only bad example but somehow the cause of our solidarity in sin, but in such a way that we bear our own responsibility and contribute to this collusion in sin.

This causality of Adam in conjunction with our own causality has not been adequately comprehended because of faulty understanding of a clause in verse 12d which describes it. Paul begins in verse 12 to contrast Adam with Christ, only he does not complete the comparison and the sentence breaks off after he speaks only of Adam. The full comparison will be picked up twice, in verses 15-17 and in verses 18-19, with the last verses being almost a restatement and then completion of verse 12: "Then as one man's trespass led to condemnation for all men, so one man's act of righteousness leads to acquittal and life for all men. For as by one man's disobedience many were made sinners, so by one man's obedience many will be made righteous." In any case, when

Paul first begins his comparison in verse 12, he feels the need to clarify his claim that we are truly affected by Adam's sin, and so he digresses in verses 12c-d and in verses 13-14. The beginning of the digression brings us to the misunderstood clause. After Paul affirms, in verse 12a-b, the Jewish tradition that sin and death indeed entered the world through "the one man," Adam, he then clarifies that tradition, specifying in verse 12c that all feel the effects of this sin ("death spread to all"). The debate arises over what Paul further specifies in verse 12d about all sinning.

While there are several possible translations, two major alternatives have generally been suggested.[3] A longstanding traditional interpretation, associated with Augustine, begins that clause by translating the Greek preposition and relative pronoun *eph' ho* as "in whom" and the entire clause as "in whom all sinned." The entire verse would thereby be understood as attributing all the clauses to the "one man," so that the thought pattern would read: "Therefore as sin came into the world through one man and death through sin, and so death spread to all (also through the one man) in whom all sinned." In this translation, we have a reaffirmation of the fact that somehow Adam's sin is ours, but in such a way that our own responsibility is not affirmed as well. This gave rise to Augustine's theory of original sin as a quasibiological inheritance, as if we somehow inherited the effects of the personal sin of Adam as our own. In popular imagination this came to be the "black mark on the soul," which needed to be washed away by baptism. While such a theory and imagination express some solidarity in sin in the human race, the images are still very much of discrete individuals who all relate to Adam but not very much to each other. The images fail to account enough for the social and communal dimensions of human collusion in sin.

Recent scholarship has generally rejected this translation as less likely grammatically (Paul would have said *en ho* if he had wanted to say "in whom") and structurally ("through the one man," which "in whom" would modify, is too far away in the sentence).

---

[3]See C. E. B. Cranfield, *Romans: A Shorter Commentary* (Grand Rapids, Mich.: William B. Eerdmans Publishing Co., 1985) 113–114.

The more likely translation of *eph' ho* is "given the fact that" or "because." While there may be some nuance of difference between these two terms, they both affirm, along with Adam's influence, that human beings share responsibility for sin and its consequences: Sin and death came into the world through one man, but "death spread to all because (or given the fact that) all sinned." This translation has given rise to theories of original sin which emphasize it as a different kind of sin, as a climate or atmosphere of sin which is internalized by every human being born into the world and which begins from the first human beings but is sustained by each individual who contributes to this atmosphere by his or her own sin.

Without going into detail or nuancing the theories, we can see for our purposes that they at least highlight in Paul what modern thought would further elaborate and describe as the social and communal dimensions of sin. Sin is not only a power or force giving rise to our own rebellion, our missing the target, but it gives rise as well to a climate of rebellion and alienation. While racial prejudice, mob violence, and oppressive economic and political structures involve individual culpability, they cannot be blamed totally on one individual. Yet they are realities. They grow out of personal choices, but they then take on a life of their own. They influence each of us into attitudes and actions which constitute our own sinfulness and which in turn reinforce the sinful structures to make them even more oppressive and alienating. Left to our own resources we are trapped in this vicious circle which began with the first human beings but has been enlarging ever since. Atonement will be the work of somehow undoing this situation, but that means a work which eliminates not only personal sin but sin in its social and communal structures.

Sin as Transgression of Law

What Paul introduced in verse 12, he makes more explicit in verses 13-14. At the same time, these verses introduce us to the relationship of law to sin. We will first see how the verses restate the point of verse 12. Then we will develop the theme of law.

> [13]Sin indeed was in the world before the law was given, but sin is not counted where there is no law. [14]Yet death reigned from Adam to Moses, even over those whose sins were not like the *transgression [parabasis]* of Adam, who was a type of the one who was to come (Rom 5:13-14).

In these verses Paul completes his digression to clarify the effect that Adam had on our sinful condition. Interpretations of these verses range between the same two general possibilities as those we presented for verse 12. Some see these verses as reaffirming that death (and related consequences of sin) comes from Adam's sin in distinction from our own. Others see these verses as affirming Adam's causality, but in conjunction with our own collusion. Much hinges on the meaning of *ouk ellogeitai* ("not counted") in verse 13. Is it "not counted" in the sense of "not clearly labeled" or "not registered with full clarity," or is it "not counted" as "not imputed" or "not attributed at all"?

To understand Paul's point, one must appreciate what he says about law. To anticipate what we will presently develop, Paul believes that Mosaic Law exposes sin with clarity and thereby makes sin even more sinful. Thus, unless one has a law, one cannot fully reckon sin as sin. This role of law would pose some obstacles to Paul's statements in verse 12, but the nature of the obstacle would vary, depending on how one translates *eph' ho* in verse 12. This leads us to the debate over the meaning of "not counted," and the two interpretations of verses 13-14. If verse 12 means that we all sin in Adam ("in whom all sinned"), then verses 13-14 would clarify this (in paraphrased form): "Sin indeed existed *objectively* from the beginning, but before the Mosaic Law it could *not be subjectively imputed* as sin. Yet, the effects of sin (death) were felt even before Mosaic Law. In that case, the effects came because of the one to whom sin could be imputed, namely, Adam, who had a law and whose transgression was therefore different from the nonimputed sins of his descendants before Moses."

We have seen, however, that the meaning of verse 12 is probably otherwise. This would lead to another interpretation of verses 13-14 and to understanding "not counted" as "not labeled." Thus (again in paraphrase): "Sin indeed existed *even as subjectively imputed* from the beginning, though before the Mosaic Law it could *not be labeled* as sin. Indeed, the effects of sin (death) were felt even before Mosaic Law. This could only be because all sinned and there was truly sin in the world, even if the sin was not labeled as such and was therefore different from sin as formal transgression of the law, as was Adam's.'' This latter interpretation seems more likely, not only because it continues the more likely translation of verse 12, but because it also continues the thought of chapters 1 and 2 of Romans, where Paul says that the Gentiles are truly as sinful as the Israelites, even though their sin is different and only Israelites with law can label sin as transgression. Thus, verses 13-14 reaffirm in their own way the social dimensions of sin and the collusion that we all share in the climate of evil that provokes sin and leads to death. This is a collusion that goes all the way back to human origins, even before the Mosaic Law. We cannot blame an Adam alone, though he shares causality, but we must acknowledge our own contribution to these social dimensions of human sinfulness for which we need atonement.

These verses introduce us likewise to another topic important for Paul, that of the law and its role of turning sin into transgression. In the verses we have been considering, the apostle says that Adam's sin is different from others without law because his sin can also be called transgression. Paul intimates that law somehow is an accomplice to sin and has negative qualities. We must be careful, however, to distinguish law from sin, in that law is not evil of its nature in the way that sin is. Paul is himself the first to tell us that "law is holy, and the commandment is holy and just and good" (Rom 7:12). He tells us that the law was "ordained by angels" (Gal 3:19) and that it "promised life" (Rom 7:10). It was a gift given by God so that those who kept it in Israel could achieve their destiny of a life in union with God. Thus, Paul quotes Leviticus 18:5: "He who does them shall live by them" (Gal 3:12). Indeed, the law was a special privilege given to Israel whereby it could live an upright life: "The Jews are entrusted with the oracles of God" (Rom 3:2). "To them belong the sonship, the glory, the covenants, the giving of the law, the worship, and the promises" (Rom 9:4). Paul even quotes law approvingly in his arguments, e.g., in 1 Corinthians 8:8-12.

Nevertheless, while the law is good in itself, it fosters evil possibilities and, because of human sinfulness, ends up with negative consequences. Paul, more than anyone else in the New Testament, develops these negative dimensions of law because of the context of his history. Christians of Jewish background were intent on reverting to Jewish law as substitute for faith in Christ or were pushing to impose Jewish law on Gentiles converting to Christianity. As a means of correcting these views, Paul shows how law, while it is good in itself, has a negative side to it and will not, therefore, be adequate as the means of proper living and human goodness.

Obviously, the first negative element of law is that it requires implementation. Israel's problem is that while it had the law, it did not keep the law and so remained in sin, as did the Gentiles who had no specially revealed law. Paul develops this point in Romans 2: "For it is not the hearers of the law who are righteous before God, but the doers of the law who will be justified. . . . You who boast in the law, do you dishonor God by breaking the law?" (vv. 13, 23). The same theme is struck in Galatians 5:3: "I testify again to every man who receives circumcision that he is bound to keep the whole law."

Paul's theology of law, however, runs more deeply than this. Paul teaches that law has some inbuilt shortcomings which actually encourage sin within us. His thinking evolves out of what we have already presented as his teaching about sin as an interior attitude or stance. Sin precedes law, and sinful persons use the reality of law to deepen their sinful attitudes and worsen their state of sin. In Paul's terms, law is personified as well as sin. The character "Sin" inhabits "Everyone" and works its dominion over him or her. It is on stage before "Law" but calls on Law as an accomplice. Law enters on stage as a weak creature, planning originally to help Everyone against Sin, but becoming quickly a lackey of Sin and another petty tyrant helping Sin kill Everyone.

When those with sinful attitudes take advantage of law to deepen their sinful stance, then sin becomes "transgression" (*parabasis*), i.e., a breaking of the law. This both confirms the nature of sin as essentially an interior state or condition and law as an accomplice, and it gives a somewhat different cast to the way popular mentality often paints its picture of sin. Many people begin with law as the first reality and then define sin as essentially the breaking of the law. Such a definition encourages a legalism which centers on sin as action and often contributes to the poor image of God's justice as rewarding or punishing on the basis of our legal standing. Beginning with sin as transgression of law also encourages a view of sin as quasi-automatic, as if there were some guilt once the action is posited, no matter what the attitude behind it. Witness the feeling of guilt that people sometimes have about missing Mass on Sunday, even though they may have had a legitimate reason. Sometimes the stress on transgression leads people to think that sin can be determined purely by external criteria or by other persons. Witness the people who ask a priest or a teacher whether they "committed a sin." While obviously priest and teacher can give insights into what constitutes serious matter for sin, they cannot get into one's conscience and motivation to determine whether one actually sinned. Beginning with sin as transgression also gives the impression that God gave the law as a contract to punish those who did not keep it, rather than that God gave law to help his people respond to him and not reject the gifts which he had already offered.

Paul's mind is otherwise. Sin does not begin as transgression, but ends that way, when it abuses the very gift of law and turns it into a tool for further sin. To make his point about the deeper meaning of sin and its existence prior to law, Paul distinguishes, in Romans 5, two different epochs in history, the epoch from Adam to Moses and the epoch from Moses to Christ. The first epoch is characterized by sin as a rebellious stance, in all the ways we have described it above. Only with Moses does God give his law, and so only in the second epoch do we see sin become transgression. (The situation of Adam himself constitutes an exception in the first epoch, since Adam had a specific commandment in the garden, so that his sin would also be transgression.) Thus, sin becomes a more and more powerful force within humanity until, when the law comes, it thwarts and then twists the very purpose of this gift from God, and then shows itself even more obviously in its heinousness by full manifestation in all the actions that law came precisely to forbid. The first two epochs then look for the third, the epoch of Christ, in order to be rescued from this sad condition. Before we look at the atoning work of Christ, let us look now in more detail at how sin twists the purpose of law and makes law its accomplice for evil.[4]

Law's Negative Role with Sin

> If it had not been for the law, I should not have known sin. I should not have known what it is to covet if the law had not said, "You shall not covet" (Rom 7:7).

One of the ways in which Paul shows law as an accomplice of sin is by describing law as itself an occasion of sin. Paul says that a good law ends up with negative results because it suggests evil that would not have otherwise been thought of. The intention of the law, certainly, is not to promote evil, and when it mentions sinful actions or attitudes, it is precisely to proscribe such things. But sin, which already dwells in a person, remains stronger than the law and uses the law as another means to perpetuate the sinful enterprise. The sinful person hears the evil that law forbids, and twists the good intention of law by hearing only another suggestion for sin.

Paul could, of course, have used an example of any law to illustrate his point. In fact, the more specific the law, the more it would have been an example of sinful action perhaps not thought of by a sinful person. But that raises the interesting question of why Paul selected "You shall not covet" as the example. Is not such a law very general rather than specific? Does not such a law forbid something that people would realize as sinful even without a law, so that this command serves as a poor example of law suggesting further evil? Why does Paul hit on the example of covetousness? It is possible that Paul uses this example to evoke the

---

[4]For an overview of Paul's theology of law, see Joseph A. Fitzmyer, S. J., "Paul and the Law," in Michael J. Taylor, ed., *A Companion to Paul: Readings in Pauline Theology* (New York: Alba House, 1975) 73–87.

image of Adam and his desire to be like God.[5] This would show the problem of sin and the weakness of law as part of the human condition from the very beginning, even though it would take until the time of Moses for the problem of law to surface in Jewish law.

Another possible reason for this example is that Paul is using the most general description of sin to show law's powerlessness against any kind of sin. "You shall not covet" is, of course, not just a reference to Adam's coveting, but is related to the Ten Commandments. Sometimes Jewish tradition summed up all the commandments as "not coveting," and described sin as "desire." Paul reflects this tendency in several places. In Romans 6:12, he warns, "Let not sin therefore reign in your mortal bodies, to make you obey their passions [literally, 'desire']." In 1 Corinthians 10:6, he describes the rebellious Israelites in the desert as the typology of sinners and gives them as warning to Christians about sin: "These things are warnings for us, not to *desire evil* as they did." In summing up sin in this way, Paul reminds us again of its social dimensions. It starts off as unhealthy egocentricity, a selfishness which desires everything for self. This self-centeredness leads one to distort the meaning and value of everyone and everything around, so that they become but objects of one's desires, thus either giving oneself too much importance or giving other parts of creation exaggerated importance for self.

We are back to what Paul said about sin being the turning away from the Creator to the creature and about this turning away leading to injustice and broken social relations. Perhaps that is why Paul describes the rebellious Israelites who "desired evil" as "idolaters" (1 Cor 6:7). In bringing commands against "coveting," the law was to be a help for both Adam and for Israel against egocentricity and the social injustice that flowed from it. Unfortunately, the self-centeredness, the sin in humanity, was so strong that it thwarted the good purposes of law and took law's prohibition of self-centeredness as another occasion for reinforcing these stances.

---

[5]Stanislas Lyonnet and Leopold Sabourin, *Sin, Redemption and Sacrifice: A Biblical and Patristic Study*, Analecta Biblica, vol. 48 (Rome: Biblical Institute Press, 1970) 53.

> [8]Apart from the law sin lies dead. [9]I was once alive apart from the law, but when the commandment came, sin revived and I died; [10]the very commandment which promised life proved to be death to me. [11]For sin, finding opportunity in the commandment, deceived me and by it killed me (Rom 7:8-11).

Related to the first weakness of law and intensifying that weakness is another way in which law becomes an occasion of sin. Paul says law not only suggests evil, it entices or sometimes provokes evil. Biblical scholars often describe Paul's thought here as indicating the psychology of "forbidden fruit." Nothing is more desirable than what one cannot have. In the same way, nothing raises one's sense of self-righteousness and one's spirit of independence more than an order not to do something. Thus, law becomes an unwitting occasion for sin to assert itself more strongly. In Romans 7:8-11, Paul gives a vivid description of this scenario. Sin precedes law and is already within us, that spirit of rebellion or self-centeredness. However, it lies dormant. Paul says it is even dead within us, i.e., it is not actively functioning. We do not consistently show rebellion or selfishness. But when law comes along and forbids something, then sin wakes up or comes to life again. The law raises our dander. It gives us a target against which to show our rebellion or to demonstrate our ego.

The law, in saying precisely what it is supposed to say, and in being good in itself, becomes the unwitting occasion of provoking our sinfulness. This entire process is illustrated so clearly in the example of the little child who is not doing anything wrong until mother says not to trample the flowers in the garden. The command becomes the occasion of suggesting something the child had not thought of and, even worse, of giving the child occasion to assert its independence and self-will by doing exactly what it is told not to do. We are like the little child with a spirit of sin that "comes alive" when law enters the scene. What we have been extracting from Romans 7:8-11 is also anticipated in the earlier verse 5, where Paul says, "While we were living in the flesh, our sinful passions, aroused by the law, were at work in our members to bear fruit for death."

Did that which is good, then, bring death to me? By no means! It was sin, working death in me through what is good, in order that sin might be shown to be sin, and through the commandment might become sinful beyond measure (Rom 7:13).

As he proceeds in chapter 7, Paul builds up a further case for his negative role of law as an accomplice of sin. In verse 13 he highlights what is, perhaps, the deepest failure of law, its making sin "more sinful" by exposing it to clear light of day for what it is and thereby making our decisions more willfully wrong when we choose it nonetheless. Biblical scholars describe this role of law as removing ignorance and imputing guilt.

The law, first of all, removes ignorance by naming sin for what it is: "Sin might be shown to be sin." Before the law came along, we were indeed already sinful people, but we always had one last good excuse. We could always plead ignorance and claim that we did not realize how wrong something was. Law removed that last good excuse. In removing that last excuse, the law also removed the last thing that might lessen culpability. Thus, the law not only removed ignorance but also increased our guilt; sin became "sinful beyond measure." This thought of Paul echoes throughout his writing. He anticipates his full explanation in Romans 3:20: "Through the law comes knowledge of sin"; in 5:13: "Sin is not counted where there is no law"; in 5:20: "Law came in to increase the trespass." He anticipates the same points by earlier letters as well. In 2 Corinthians 3:6-7, he describes the written code as that which "kills" and as a "dispensation of death." In Galatians 3:10, he says the law ends up being a curse. Law requires that we obey all of it. We do not, so the law renders us more guilty and thereby cursed.

> [24]The law was our custodian until Christ came, that we might be justified by faith. [25]But now that faith has come, we are no longer under a custodian; for in Christ Jesus you are all sons of God, through faith (Gal 3:24-25).

In this section of Galatians Paul adds one further insight into the weakness of law which he does not make explicit in Romans. Paul here speaks of the temporary nature of Jewish law. He likens it to a custodian, literally in Greek, *paidagōgos*. A *paidagōgos* was a slave in a family who was responsible for the children for as long as they were minors. When the children reached maturity, then the role of the *paidagōgos* was no longer necessary. Paul makes analogy to the law. The law was to care for us until we reached maturity in Christ. It served a commendable function. It taught us morality; its commands could at least check sin and hold us in line better than if we remained lawless. But its role was always preparatory for maturity in Christ, and it yielded its place once Christ came and brought us this new life.

Actually, there might be a more negative cast even to this temporary role of law. From all that we have seen, law was not temporary simply because its time would run out. It was temporary because it could not adequately achieve its role. While it was better than nothing, it did not have the power to achieve its purposes. Sin was too powerful. Law needed the arrival of a better teacher who could effectively move us out of sin by overcoming its power. Thus, Paul precedes his section on the *paidagōgos* with this observation: "If a law had been given which could make alive, then righteousness would indeed be by the law. But the scripture consigned all things to sin, that what was promised to faith in Jesus Christ might be given to those who believe" (vv. 21-22).

To sum up all of this theology of law, we might say that the biggest problem with law is that it remains external to human beings. It can tell one what to do, but it cannot move one interiorly to do it. Because of this limitation and given the countervailing power of sin in humanity, the role of law became its weakness. It was to teach and to exhort to moral behavior. Instead, it became an accomplice of sin, suggesting evil, provoking one to evil, exposing evil in such a way as to make our choices more blatantly rebellious and self-serving and, finally, making us more guilty than before law came along. "Law" ends up as a second character in Paul's morality play, along with "Sin," leaving "Everyone" in need of atonement. It is no wonder, with the way that law cooperates with sin, that Paul sometimes uses another word to describe sin, namely, *anomia,* or "lawlessness" (cf. Rom 6:19 and 2 Cor 6:14).

Spiritual Death

In Paul's morality play a third character enters center stage as an accomplice of Sin and Law. Death is personified by Paul and completes the defeat of Everyone, who is already shackled by Sin with the help of Law. When Death joins its accomplices, we have the full scene showing why the human race needs atonement through Christ. Death, as ruling tyrant, establishes the final situation from which Christ needs to rescue humanity: "The last enemy to be destroyed is death" (1 Cor 15:26). In considering this last enemy and in trying to understand Paul's intention, a number of questions arise. Is Paul talking about physical death or spiritual death? Is it an effect of sin or a natural consequence? Is it now or later? Paul's theology of death is actually quite multi-faceted, and what we now consider will illustrate the richness of his thought.[6]

> Do you not know that if you yield yourselves to any one as obedient slaves, you are slaves of the one whom you obey, either of sin, which leads to death, or of obedience, which leads to righteousness? (Rom 6:16).

This passage of Romans indicates that one meaning of death for Paul is that of spiritual death. In this particular verse death is contrasted with righteousness, so that it becomes a description of unrighteousness. What this means in detail will be clearer after we have considered righteousness in the last chapter. In general, we have the sense that "death" here is a metaphorical term indicating a breakdown in relationships as a result of sinful attitudes. A helpful way of arriving at this specific meaning of death for Paul is to recognize it as contrast to "life," defined in spiritual or qualitative terms. In English we have two ways of speaking about life, namely, biological and psychological or social ways. We can say that one has life, meaning biological function, i.e., that one is breathing, etc. We can, however, refer to life as a quality of the biologically functioning individual, i.e., to say that he

---

[6]For a summary of the topic see J. Christiaan Beker, *Paul the Apostle: The Triumph of God in Life and Thought* (Philadelphia: Fortress Press, 1980) 213-234.

or she has goals, meaning and relationships. In this latter sense we mean that someone is *really* alive, not just physically existing. Paul very often refers to life in this latter psychological or social way, describing quality of life. Death would then be a contrast to this kind of life. It would mean being spiritually dead, i.e., having no sense of purpose, meaning, or relationships, even if one is still biologically functioning. It would reflect what we imply when we look at someone and declare, "Boy, is that one dead!"

In analyzing Paul we are looking first at those texts where Paul highlights death as loss of meaning and loss of relationships or quality of life. A major section is Romans 5-8. Besides the text of 6:16 which we have seen, we find other passages. In 5:17 Paul personifies death in contrast to a quality of life: "If because of one man's trespass, death reigned through that one man, much more will those who receive the abundance of grace and the free gift of righteousness reign in life through the one man Jesus Christ." While this passage speaks of life as a future reality and has link also to physical death and eternal life, the previous verses show that life is a "gift of grace" which has already "abounded for many" (v. 15) and is a "free gift" bringing "justification" in the present. As life already unfolds in a qualitative sense, so it counteracts death, which would unfold already in our lives because of sin.

In 7:9-10, Paul makes obvious that life and death are qualitative terms describing a person, since he applies both realities to himself or to some hypothetical person presently alive physically: "I was once alive apart from the law, but when the commandments came, sin revived and I died; the very commandment which promised life proved to be death to me." We see here Paul also making explicit that law is a force which brings on death through its manipulation by sin, a point already made by 7:5: "Our sinful passions, aroused by the law, were at work in our members to bear fruit for death." Finally, Paul makes the same point in 8:10 about life and death as qualitative, metaphorical descriptions of present realities in persons biologically living: "If Christ is in you, although your bodies are dead because of sin, your spirits are alive because of righteousness."

To set the mind on the flesh is death, but to set the mind on the Spirit is life and peace (Rom 8:6).

Complementing these insights about spiritual death, Paul comes closest to giving us a formal definition of death in this text of Romans 8:6. Comprehension of this statement requires adequate understanding of what Paul means by "flesh" (*sarx*). This is a term for Pauline anthropology which is linked not only to death but to sin before death. What we have to say here will thus elucidate what we have said previously about sin in Paul.

We must remember, once again, that Paul is not always consistent in the meaning he gives to words. He also uses more words for his anthropology than the ones we now consider. Nevertheless, allowing for exceptions and additional developments, we may safely say (1) that Paul has three major words to describe human beings, "body, spirit, and flesh" (*sōma, pneuma,* and *sarx*); and (2) for Paul these terms do not describe parts of a human being, but the entire human person from different perspectives or in different contexts. More than anything else these words are relational terms, putting the social context around human personality. They say implicitly that human beings are social by nature. The broadest term is *sōma* (body), which may be defined as the entire person insofar as he or she is capable of relationships and is able to contact the world outside self. While Paul may sometimes intend "body" to mean simply the physical part of a human being (2 Cor 4:10) or may use "body" pejoratively as a synonym for his word "flesh" (Rom 8:10), more often he intends the word to mean "the self." Scholars have been accustomed to saying that for Paul a person does not *have* a body, but rather *is* a body. By and large, the term is a neutral description allowing the possibility of the self to move into good relationships or evil, to become a "body of sin" (Rom 6:6) or a body "holy and acceptable to God" (Rom 12:1).

The words *pneuma* (spirit) and *sarx* (flesh) describe the qualities of the relationships of the self. "Spirit" denotes the entire person insofar as he or she is turned toward what is meaningful, what confirms and creates human life and existence. This turn of the person toward what is truly enhancing incorporates rational insight and thoughtful moral choices based on human nature, so that "spirit" in Paul may sometimes be equated with *psychē* (living person) and would mean a person fully alive and not just biologically existing (1 Thess 5:23). However, since the relationship that is ultimately meaningful and that ultimately creates and confirms our being is the relationship to God, "spirit" denotes the entire person insofar as he or she is turned toward God. That is why it is often difficult and sometimes impossible to distinguish the human "spirit" from the divine "Spirit" that indwells and gives final meaning to human existence.

Sarx (flesh) is the opposite of *pneuma*. While "flesh" may sometimes mean simply the physical part of a person (2 Cor 4:11) or may sometimes be a neutral term for "self," a synonym for *sōma* (Gal 1:16; Rom 6:19), most often it implies the entire person insofar as he or she is turned away from God and toward creaturely existence. "Flesh" implies not only that we have a weak side and a natural frailty as created beings, but that we also sometimes cater to that weak side and give it an importance that it ought not to have. Turning toward self and to all creatures as means for exalting self is in reality a distortion of all relationships and is, in fact, a breakdown of true relationship with God, others, and self. It is self-destructive in the long run. With this context for "flesh," we can better understand Paul's definition of death as "setting the mind on the flesh." Turning toward self and others in a distorted way is to turn away from God, a description of sin in Paul as we have described it previously. Thus, sin dwells in the flesh (Rom 7:5, 14; 8:3). Now, when one turns away from God, one thereby cuts self off from God, so that sin, which comes from living in the flesh, bears fruit for death (Rom 7:5). "Setting the mind on the flesh," then, is not just turning from God but is entering a state or condition whereby one is cut off from God. Death for Paul is, in the first instance, a separation from God.

We must complete our definition, however, because more can be said about both sin and flesh. Our previous consideration of sin showed a strong emphasis on the social dimensions as well as individual. Sin, which turns one against God, also turns one against neighbor and leads to the breakdown of proper social structures and relationships. We must now add that for Paul, this is one of the dimensions of "living in the flesh" and is another reason why he says that sin dwells in the flesh. In Galatians 5:19-21 Paul describes the "works of the flesh": "fornication, impurity, licentiousness, idolatry, sorcery, enmity, strife, jealousy, anger, selfishness, dissension, party spirit, envy, drunkenness, carousing, and the like." This list gives an excellent overview of all that we have been saying about "flesh." Some of the sins highlight a turning away from God. Others describe a distorted view of and a turning toward self. Others show that "sins of the flesh" do not refer simply to the material side of a person, nor do they show Paul having an excessive preoccupation with sexual matters, as some Christians think. Certainly, the physical is included, because it is part of our human condition and can be distorted as well as any other part. Nevertheless, "living in the flesh" depicts more than these areas of life. Many of Paul's examples are quite spiritual or nonmaterial in nature and include the whole person. In the long run, most of the works of the flesh, like those of sin which we gave earlier on, highlight distorted social relationships and the use and abuse of others for one's own interests. "Living in the flesh," then, is not only to turn from God, but to turn from proper relations to self and others. Now, when one turns from all of this, one thereby cuts self off from one's true self and from others as well as from God. "He who sows to his own flesh will from the flesh reap corruption" (Gal 6:8). "To set the mind on the flesh," then, is to enter a state of being separated not only from God but also from true self and from others. "Death" is qualitative psychological and social death to the fullest.

Physical Death

"O death, where is thy sting?" The sting of death is sin (1 Cor 15:55-56).

Having shown that death for Paul puts strong emphasis on spiritual or psychological and social dimensions, we must nevertheless observe that Paul also brings physical death into his concept. This is because the reality of death in human existence is complex and ambiguous, because the Old Testament has a multi-faceted approach to the subject, and because Paul carries all this background to its deepest dimensions.[7]

Human experience encounters death in a complex and ambivalent way. On the one hand, it is a natural and expected part of life. We are all creatures and are destined to die as part of creaturely existence. On the other hand, death is a wrenching experience, to put it mildly, an end to all projects and relationships, the final—and successful—threat to our very selves. Thus, while we may embrace death as logical and inevitable, death is also enemy. At best, death in human experience is an enigmatic problem.

The Old Testament is quite aware of this enigma. It assumes death as normal and natural and does not treat it always with hostility. Even the ideal final time of salvation will include death: "No more shall there be in it [Jerusalem of the final times] an infant that lives but a few days, or an old man who does not fill out his days, for the child shall die a hundred years old" (Isa 65:20). The Old Testament is hardly preoccupied at all with natural physical death, but much more with that death as it relates to meaningful life and relationships. Thus, it dwells much more on the spiritual or psychological and social dimensions of death as we described this in the previous section. However, this emphasis on meaningful life and death does incorporate physical dimensions as well, since physical death can be a help or a hindrance to this quality of life. Thus, the Old Testament sees as evil a premature death or a violent physical death or one in which there are no heirs, because any of these circumstances diminishes the quality of life or the full enjoyment of life in community.

In the same vein, instead of moving from physical death as it contributes to spiritual death, we can also move the other way around. There are some kinds of physical death that can be attributed to a sinful life or a sinful society. Dissolute living brings its consequences sometimes in weakened health and even in death: "Fools die for lack of sense" (Prov 10:21) and "He who is stead-

---

[7]See Lloyd R. Bailey, Sr., *Biblical Perspectives on Death*, Overtures to Biblical Theology (Philadelphia: Fortress Press, 1979).

fast in righteousness will live, but he who pursues evil will die"
(Prov 11:19). The same on a communal level. The prophets
predicted that Israel would be destroyed by invading armies not
because God was sending a merely extrinsic sign that sin had to
be eliminated but because Israel's injustice weakened the fibre of
the community and opened it even to physical death. Psychoso-
matic illness and the intrinsic effects of sinful social structures
show that it is not inaccurate to say that even physical death is
sometimes a consequence of sin.

The text that devotes most attention to death as consequence
of sin is, of course, Genesis 2–3. It is not clear just what the condition of humanity was before the Fall, and theologians still debate whether we would have been immortal had there been no
sin. Certainly, the "tree of life" could signify quality of life and
leave open the question of physical immortality. In any case, our
concrete situation now after the Fall is that of a sinful humanity
that experiences death. While loss of the "tree of life" may mean
spiritual death, the reference to Adam's returning to "the dust
of the earth" in Genesis 3:19b includes physical death as well.
It may very well be that we would have died anyway, since we
"are dust," but now our return to dust is in the context of toil
and suffering with physical death as final stage of that reality:
"In the sweat of your face you shall eat bread till you return to
the ground, for out of it you were taken" (Gen 3:19a).

With the theology of Genesis 2–3, biological death takes on
predominantly a role as enemy, closely associated with sin and
seen as consequence of sin. It is not necessarily the case that physical death is purely and simply a consequence of sin, but that physical death has become another *kind* of death because of the
entrance of sin into our world. Death is certainly different for
us, whether we would or would not have died in a sinless world.
The Old Testament evolves in this negative view of death until,
finally, apocalyptic imagery at the end of the Old Testament
describes death in both its aspects, metaphorical and biological,
as a power to be conquered. In this instance biological death is
included insofar as it is touched by human sin but also insofar
as it contains threat and anxiety as an enigma of human existence.
Nevertheless, even apocalyptic expresses the ambiguity of human

relationship with death. While it poses death as enemy, it also affirms that some deaths are a blessing, e.g., releasing one from great suffering or bearing witness for a just cause as a martyr. It also says that death is a problem only for the wicked, whereas the just face death with courage and the conviction that it is not ultimate.

Paul elaborates his teaching on death in the background of apocalyptic thought. Thus, while death for him is spiritual death or separation from God, self, and others, it is also part of a total reality or power that includes physical death as consequence of sin. In fact, for Paul the connection of physical death with sin becomes a much stronger point than it was in the Old Testament. In Romans 5 and in 1 Corinthians 15, Paul makes his own the story of Genesis 3: "In Adam all die" (1 Cor 15:22). In these passages the death which came into the world includes physical death. Physical death should have been normal and natural, if it existed at all in creation as God intended it. But now sin has given it new dimensions. Insofar as physical death confirms and seals one's separation from God, it is a consequence—and indeed the final consequence—of sin. As Paul puts it in the text introducing this section, it is sin that gives death its "sting," i.e., that makes death a negative experience and an enemy to be overcome.

Ultimately, it is better not to separate the physical and the metaphorical dimensions of death in its relationship to sin and law in Paul. For the apostle, physical death is but the finishing touches of a long process that has already begun in the sinner. "The end of these things [of sin] is death" (Rom 6:21); that is, the goal toward which all sin is headed and the final point at which it arrives is death. But one already experiences the start of this death in this world. In Romans 6:23, two verses after the one just cited, Paul says, "The wages of sin is death." Now wages are not paid all at once, but are doled out periodically and regularly. One who turns away from God in sin begins the process of separation bit by bit, until physical death becomes the end point. Thus, as final conclusion we may say that death becomes the third element, along with sin and law, controlling that world for which Christ must make atonement. This death is a total power, with both present and future reality, with a spiritual and physical dimension, and "the last enemy to be destroyed" (1 Cor 15:26).

3

The Means of Atonement

The previous chapter has shown the world without Christ, a world locked in sin and death with law reinforcing their dominion. Now we can see what Christ needs to rescue us from, and so we turn to Paul's description of the process of atonement understood in the broadest sense of the term. In this chapter we are concerned with *how* Christ atones. In the next chapter we will elaborate *what* that work ultimately achieves in us and in our world.

Atonement Through Christ's Death and Resurrection

> [8]For [Christ's] sake I have suffered the loss of all things, and count them as refuse, in order that I may gain Christ [9]and be found in him, not having a righteousness of my own, based on law, but that which is through faith in Christ, the righteousness from God that depends on faith; [10]that I may know him and the power of his resurrection, and may share his sufferings, becoming like him in his death, [11]that if possible I may attain the resurrection from the dead. [12]Not that I have already obtained this or am already perfect; but I press on to make it my own, because Christ Jesus has made me his own (Phil 3:8-12).

This passage serves as a good introduction to our chapter, since it highlights what is important about Christ for Paul and thus begins to show Paul's vision of Christianity. In showing that the importance of Christ is to bring a righteousness from God through Christ's death and resurrection, the text also highlights atonement in the broad sense, describing one of the goals of Christ's saving work as well as the means. Paul's vision of Christianity is thus centered on a theology of atonement. We will see, however, as we give more detail to his teaching, that Paul's vision is not identical with what I have been calling "the popular view of atonement."

As I indicated above, we will leave consideration of the goal or effects of atonement for the next chapter, and so we postpone consideration of our righteousness or justification until then. For now we point out that besides the word "righteousness," there is also the phrase "righteousness from God," which helps us understand the "justice of God" as we discussed it in chapter 1. Because of the difference in prepositions, the phrases are not identical. Nevertheless, the former gives us hints about the latter, supporting what we said previously, namely, that "justice of God" is both power and gift. There are hints that the justice of God is a subjective genitive, a power, for here in this passage justice or righteousness is described as "from God," i.e., as God's possession to begin with and not Paul's ("not having a righteousness of my own"). It seems, though, also an objective genitive, a gift, for it achieves something in Paul ("but [having] righteousness from God"). God's justice here, at any rate, is not primarily a static attribute of God, nor simply God's judging us, but a gift manifesting positive saving activity "from God."

God's justice is experienced through faith, i.e., a perception of God's revealed activity and trusting acceptance of God's gift. Moreover, since that justice is manifest through Christ, faith becomes the perception of what God has done in Christ and trusting acceptance of the way in which Christ achieves this justice or righteousness. We are thus led to what I call "the means of atonement." Paul names these means in the next verses: the power of Christ's resurrection and a share in his sufferings and death. A similar description of the means of atonement is given in Romans 4:25: "Jesus our Lord . . . was put to death for our trespasses and raised for our justification." For Paul, cross and resurrection form a unity and each needs the other to be complete. We will need to discuss each phase separately to see how each contributes to the means by which Christ atones for our sins and their consequences, but it is important to keep in mind the unity of death and resurrection as one complex event.

From the text in Philippians, where the resurrection is mentioned first, we learn that the resurrection is indeed the key event making effective all of Christ's saving work. While further texts will have to show how the resurrection is effective for atonement, this text introduces the point by saying that the resurrection has power. This power of the resurrection is multifaceted.[1] It shows God's power in being able to raise Jesus from the dead. It shows Christ with the new power of his own risen state. But it also endows Christ with new power as a life-giving force, enabling him to transform Paul and every Christian by incorporating them into his very life. We will see in more detail that atonement is achieved by the communication to us of the risen life of Christ, creating new possibilities that allow us to leave the life of sin and death under the law for a new life in Christ that unites us to God. Notice in our text the many hints of the power of the resurrection as this intimate, transforming union with the risen Christ: Paul wants to be found "in him" (v. 9), that he might "know" him (v. 10), which in the Bible means to have an intimate experience of him so that he might "become like him" (v. 10), i.e., literally "be conformed" to him, because Christ "has made him his own" (v. 12).

Participation in the risen life of Christ, however, is participation also in his suffering and death.[2] Paul says this in verse 10 where, literally, "that I may share his sufferings" is translated, "that I may know the fellowship of his sufferings." Just how one has fellowship in Christ's sufferings is not spelled out, but this verse gives some hints that will be made more explicit in other texts to be analyzed. Certainly there is some sense for Paul that

[1] Joseph A. Fitzmyer, S.J., *To Advance the Gospel: New Testament Studies* (New York: Crossroad, 1981) 202-217, especially 208-209.

[2] See Barnabas Ahern, C.P., "The Fellowship of His Sufferings," in Michael J. Taylor, S.J., ed., *A Companion to Paul: Readings in Pauline Theology* (New York: Alba House, 1975) 37-64.

suffering must be borne for the cause of Christ (2 Cor 6:3-10). There is also a sense of imitation of Christ (1 Thess 1:6). In both these cases the stress on the risen life of Christ is as a future reality. Paul and every Christian gets there by going the same route that Christ did, through death to resurrection. Verse 11 seems to indicate this in making resurrection a future reality, an eschatological event. Verse 12 says explicitly that we have not yet attained the perfection that comes with final resurrection from the dead. But Paul seems to intend more than this.

For one thing, Paul is scarcely interested in any of his writings about the historical Jesus and the past events of that earthly life, so it is not likely that he intends "fellowship in his sufferings" to mean merely a resemblance between Christian life and Jesus' historical death. For another thing, Paul sandwiches this phrase in Philippians 3 between statements that show participation in the risen life of Christ as having already begun, even while it is true that we do not yet share fully in the resurrection. The verbs "to gain [Christ]" in verse 8, and "to be found [in him]" in verse 9, as well as "to know [him]" in verse 10 are all in the aorist tense to indicate action already beginning, for which Paul counts all else as trash. Each verb has the sense of "to begin to." Moreover, as we indicated above, all these statements, along with "the power of his resurrection" hint at an intimate transforming union with Christ. It would seem, then, that "fellowship of his sufferings" refers also to a real union with Christ whereby his very suffering and death is source of our own. One final confirmation of this comes from Paul's adding to "fellowship of his sufferings" the phrase "becoming like him in his death." Literally, this says, "being conformed [or co-figured] to his death" and is a word coined by Paul, along with words like "to co-suffer," "to be co-buried," "to be co-glorified" (Rom 6:4; 8:17). Now if some words express the Christian's inner union with Christ's resurrection, then the other words must express inner union with his death.

In anticipation of other texts, we can venture an introductory explanation of how, though Christ's death as history remains past, one is joined to Christ's death as part of his saving activity—as part of what I call the means of atonement. This occurs because the death has continuity and is incorporated into the risen life of Christ. This can happen in two interrelated ways. On the one hand, Christ's resurrection is one event with his death as conquest. In his death Jesus appeared to be overcome by sin, law, and even death itself but was in reality refusing allegiance to any of these powers. His resurrection completed that rejection and makes it available to us as our own. As we are joined to Christ in his own risen life, we are therefore also joined to Christ in his death to sin and its related powers. We can be said to have not only a life-with-Christ, but also a death-with-Christ. From the other side of the coin, we can say that Christ's death was really the expression of a pattern of life, expressive of his entire life of love and obedience. This pattern of life never ends and is incorporated into the life of the risen Christ. This life is ours through union with the risen Christ. We can thus say that the death Jesus died is a death once and for all in the past, but the virtues with which he died, his pattern of life, is ours. By living in Christ, we are able to pattern our lives on his, even to the culminating expression of that pattern in death. We share in the death of Christ by sharing in his resurrection.

With this summary text of Philippians as our base, we must now look at Paul's writings in more detail to see how Christ frees us from sin, death, and law by the means of his death and resurrection. We must also contrast this with the popular view of the means of atonement that we have also been discussing in this study.

Sacrificial Death

A theology of the cross developed very quickly in the early Church for at least two reasons. One was that it presented a puzzle and even a scandal to the cultures within which Christianity began, and so Christians felt compelled to shed some light on this mystery. The central event for Christians was, of course, the resurrection; but belief in the risen Lord soon led the first believers to see if this event did not help them make sense out of Christ's death on a cross. The other reason for a theology of the cross was that suffering was still very much a part of Christian lives even after the resurrection. Christians needed to explain such realities through Christ's own suffering, so as not to make Christianity a naive and myopic religion, totally out of touch with this world. Thus, we find in Paul traces of an earlier Christian tradition which already drew out the positive or redemptive value of the death of Christ: "I delivered to you as of first importance what I also received, that Christ died for our sins in accordance with the scriptures" (1 Cor 15:3); "Jesus Christ . . . gave himself for our sins" (Gal 1:4).

Exactly how, of course, Christ died *for our sins* is what we need to further explore. As we do so, we will see that Paul's teaching is quite different from the popular model that we described in the introductory chapter of this book. That model of our introduction portrays Christ as "balancing the scales" in a kind of legal justice. God is seen as demanding satisfaction, and Christ is seen as undergoing punishment for sin to give that satisfaction in our place. Ultimately, in that view, the death of Christ is singled out as an isolated event which atones for sin by itself, and which does so by making Christ a penal substitute for all of humanity. There is serious question whether this description can be found anywhere in the New Testament. Certainly, it is not the best way to describe Paul's model. Presently we shall suggest that Paul's model may be better described as a representative journey in which the risen Christ invites us to participate.

> [7]One will hardly die for a righteous man—though perhaps for a good man one will dare even to die. [8]But God shows his love for us in that while we were yet sinners Christ died for us. [9]Since, therefore, we are now justified by his blood, much more shall we be saved by him from the wrath of God (Rom 5:7-9).

Paul builds on the earlier Christian theology of the cross that was already developing before him. In this passage which we have cited, he speaks of the varied effects of Christ's atonement coming from the blood of Christ, who dies for sinners. This imagery derives from the convergence of several lines of thought from the Old Testament and from Judaism of his times. One such tradition out of Judaism was that of the martyr or the just person being vindicated in death and whose death had an effect on the community of believers. In 4 Maccabees, for example, there is a story of Eleazar, an aged Jew, and of a mother and her seven children, all of whom resist Hellenistic persecution of their faith and die in martyrdom. Their death is seen as a saving death for themselves and for the community: "Because of them our enemies did not rule over our nation, the tyrant was punished, and the homeland purified—they having become, as it were, a ransom for the sin of our nation. And through the blood of those devout ones and their death as an expiation, divine Providence preserved Israel that previously had been afflicted" (17:20-22). Other texts with similar theology are found during this era of Judaism, e.g., 2 Maccabees 7, especially verses 30-38; Wisdom 3:1-9.

To this martyr theology was joined that of the Suffering Servant of Isaiah 53. As Israel understood this hymn, the Servant reflected Israel's suffering in the exile and explained why God permitted suffering in the past and seemed likely to allow it as history continued. That suffering was not a lost opportunity or simply a negative experience. It was and would be redemptive. Israel's commitment was and would be vindicated by her suffering, and that suffering would be a means of salvation for all people. Thus, a Servant is projected as coming in the final times who "was wounded for our transgressions, . . . makes himself an offering for sin, . . . [and shall] make many to be accounted righteous; and shall bear their iniquities" (Isa 53:5, 10-11). This Servant is a symbolic representation of Israel at the end time who by suffering will be a means of salvation for all. The Servant may also be an individual, but only insofar as that individual represents the community and, as a corporate personality, acts in the name of the community. This text never attained prominence for biblical Israel, nor for early Judaism during the Christian Era, and the traits of the Servant were certainly not associated with those expected of the Messiah, though the potential was there for meditation on suffering. It was the early Christian community that made much of this passage, including application of it to the image of the Messiah.

When the Christian community did focus on Isaiah 53 in the hindsight of the developing martyr theology of the Judaism of that time, they were thereby able to formulate a theology of

Christ's suffering and death as vicarious atonement, i.e., as substitutionary or representative for all humanity. This background enabled Paul to say that Christ "died for our sins." Still, there was one more ingredient to complete this theology and to help us understand how Christ is a substitute for all of us as the means of atonement. In what we have seen so far, martyr or Servant theology could imply simply giving one's life for a cause, i.e., being a moral force or a moral influence. The Old Testament wanted to say more than this. Paul and the early Christians wanted to say that Christ is more than this. The martyr or Servant actually effects a change in us. The other ingredient brought to the theology of atonement that makes this clear is the Old Testament doctrine of sacrifice.

> [24]All . . . are justified by his grace as a gift, through the redemption which is in Christ Jesus, [25]whom God put forward as an expiation (*hilastērion*) by his blood, to be received by faith (Rom 3:24-25).

The references to blood in this passage, in Romans 5:9 cited above, and in other texts all indicate that the martyr and Servant theology developed by late Judaism and/or the early Christians was understood primarily within the context of Temple sacrifice. Both Judaism and Christianity outside the Holy Land comprised communities for whom the animal sacrifices of Jerusalem were either not central or no longer operative in practice because of the distance from the Temple in Jerusalem. This did not eliminate the high significance of these institutions even for these groups, but it did lead to new considerations that influenced the thought of both Judaism and Christianity in general. Diaspora Judaism added to the ideas regarding sacrifice a spiritualized interpretation, applying the theories of sacrifice metaphorically or analogically to the lives of human beings themselves. Christians took this same approach in describing the life of Christ itself as a sacrifice. With the help of this metaphor Christians could thus show that Christ's suffering atones for sin in a manner that is deeper than just moral example, for it is truly representative or substitutionary for us. Unfortunately, however, the symbolism of sacrifice has been subject to frequent misunderstanding, still strongly argued by some,[3] so that it has been the chief culprit in erroneously presenting Christ as a *penal* substitute, "balancing the scales" for a sinful humanity.

The misperception arises out of the symbolism of the blood involved in sacrifices. It is frequently assumed that the central element of a sacrifice is the killing of the animal and that the shedding of the blood represents that death. In this view, one would be offering an animal as a substitute for self, would be indicating that one deserved death because of sin, and would thereby shed the blood of the animal as a vicarious punishment for sin in order to satisfy God's justice, conceived as demanding due punishment. One would thereby appease God, so that atonement would mean primarily this act of appeasement through the death of the animal in sacrifice. In technical terminology this has come to be called sacrifice as *propitiation* of God for sin. When applying this view of sacrifice to Christ, Christians have seen his death as the most perfect propitiation for sin. In this view, the animal sacrifices were always inadequate because they could never adequately represent the human beings for whom they symbolically substituted. Christ, however, in taking our human existence, could truly take the place of all humanity and, in shedding his blood, undergo the punishment we all deserve, satisfy God's justice, and thereby be a perfect once-for-all sacrifice for our sins.

The difficulty with this position is that it misplaces the emphasis in sacrifice on the death or the killing of the animal. Recent biblical scholarship has shown that the essence of the sacrifice was not so much in the killing of the animal as in the offering of the blood of the animal as a symbol of one's own life.[4] The text of Leviticus 17:11 is a key to this symbolism: "The life of the flesh is in the blood; and I have given it for you upon the altar to make atonement for your souls; for it is the blood that makes atonement, by reason of the life." In this text the blood

[3]Leon Morris, *The Atonement: Its Meaning and Significance* (Downers Grove, Ill.: Inter-Varsity Press, 1983) 43–67, 151–176.

[4]Robert J. Daly, S.J., *The Origins of the Christian Doctrine of Sacrifice* (Philadelphia: Fortress Press, 1978) 1–6 and 25–34.

of the animal is considered the source of the animal's life. In sacrifice the worshiper considers the animal as representing him or her and pours the blood of the animal as a symbolic gesture that the life of the animal—and the worshiper represented by the animal—is being released to be reunited with God. In this ritual the separation that has been caused by sin is thus overcome, and one is reconciled with God once again. The essence of the sacrifice, then, is in the freeing of the blood as life to return to God, not in the killing of the animal or shedding blood as death. It is true that unfortunately the animal dies when the blood is released, but that has no sacrificial meaning and is not the purpose of the sacrifice.

Atonement is not, then, appeasement of God, nor propitiating God for sin by the death of a penal substitute. When Christ's death is described as a sacrifice, it does not mean that he instead of us is punished by death in order to satisfy God's justice. Rather, it means that Christ's death is his perfect offering of his life to God, an expression of perfect obedience or perfect unity of wills, which, as representative for all humanity, enables us to move out of sin and alienation into renewed unity with God. Atonement is God's action and humanity's cooperation in reuniting humanity with God through union with Christ, whose blood released in death is sacrificial symbol of his life fully joined to God. In technical terminology this description of sacrifice as a means of atonement is called *expiation,* meaning the removal of sin for the reuniting of the person to the will of God.

There is a marked difference between sacrifice as propitiation and sacrifice as expiation. Propitiation has God as object, i.e., God as one to be placated because of sin. Expiation has God as subject and sin as object, i.e., God as the one who graciously acts to remove sin. The word "expiation" (*hilastērion*) is literally "the mercy seat," or "the place where sins are wiped out," i.e., the thronelike cover of the ark of the covenant in the holy of holies of the Temple. On the Day of Atonement in the Old Testament the priest sprinkled the blood of sacrifice on the mercy seat as a symbol of God's mercy, God's graciousness in forgiving their sin, and the consequent reconsecration of the people to God's service. There was no sense of God being angry or having to be appeased but rather a sense of positive divine concern and action toward Israel to help right what was wrong. In the same way, when Paul describes Christ in sacrificial terms, he envisions not a penal substitute but God's gift, who, in the name of all of us, lives a life of perfect unity with God and thereby reunites us all with God.

Death as Culmination of Christ's Life

[7][Christ Jesus] emptied himself, taking the form of a servant, being born in the likeness of men. [8]And being found in human form he humbled himself and became obedient unto death, even death on a cross (Phil 2:7-8).

In Paul's spiritualization of the concept of sacrifice and its application to the life of Christ we see the cross and death of Jesus in a positive light, not as punishment as popular theory of atonement often envisions them. In addition, we move away from seeing the cross and death as realities isolated from the rest of Christ's life. They are, rather, the final expression and the culminating expression of an entire life. Christ's death is the supreme example of perfect obedience to the will of God even in the midst of adversity and the mystery of human suffering. It becomes the best expression of what Jesus did during his entire life. The hymn from Philippians which we have cited describes the whole life of Christ as obedience, and says that this is true *even* unto death. The same message is given in the comparison of Christ with Adam in Romans 5. Whereas Adam's life was one of disobedience, Christ's was one of perfect obedience, which, after its supreme expression in death, becomes the means of reconciliation for all of humanity.

These texts give further support to what we said previously about the death of Christ expressing the pattern of his life. They also show the reality of Christ's death (and life) that lies under Paul's sacrificial imagery and that represents us as a spiritual sacrifice to reunite us to God. We have still to show that this representation is not substitutionary, with us remaining passive to Christ's atoning, and we have still to show that we do more than just imitate the pattern of life expressed by Christ's death.

These points await treatment of the resurrection passages. In gradually building as a model for Paul's theology of atonement— what I call a representative but also participatory journey with the risen Christ—we can from these texts expand on the representative nature of the journey, saving its participatory nature for later texts.

From what we have seen, we can affirm that Christ's death, far from being isolated from his life, is the fullest expression of that life and establishes the pattern of a life of love and obedience. In whatever way we are joined to it, it represents us in positive fashion as pattern for our own life and not as punishment to appease an angry God. If we formulate this in vocabulary that is not Paul's but is consistent with his thought, we might begin to speak of a journey of Jesus that represents us as follows: The journey begins with God's justice, conceived as a saving justice, as we have described it in chapter 1. God looks upon the human race and finds it in sin and alienation. There is no justice. No one is "doing it right." In God's fidelity to us and God's desire to make us just, God sends us Jesus to take on our human existence and to "do it right." Jesus lives perfect obedience. Paul stresses the obedience in death but implies obedience through life, a perfect human journey representative for all humanity, rejecting the disobedience and alienation brought by Adam and his descendants, as described in chapter 2. We are saved insofar as we can "do it right," dying to our old life and living this new one, i.e., leaving our own journey to be joined in some way to Christ's. We will see how Paul envisions our being joined to Christ through the power of the resurrection, but first we must elaborate on some further dimensions of Christ's death as expressing a pattern of life.

> [1]The churches of Macedonia . . . [3]gave according to their means, as I can testify, and beyond their means. . . . [7]Now . . . see that you excel in this gracious work also. . . . [9]For you know the grace of our Lord Jesus Christ, that though he was rich, yet for your sake he became poor, so that by his poverty you might become rich (2 Cor 8:1-9).

Christ's "doing it right" includes a communal dimension of his life that is expressed by his death as well. Recalling that sin is not only distorted attitude but also the breakdown of social relationships, the oppression of people, an immoral climate, and solidarity in evil, we can recognize Christ's life as never yielding to that kind of social distortion and, in fact, as embodying the opposite pattern of life. His death bears final witness to that communal orientation of Christ's life. He is killed for criticizing the power structures of his time, for consorting with those on the margins of society, for preaching good news to the poor that effects changes beginning even in this world and that demands the change of social structures along with conversion of heart.

This social dimension of Christ's life is prominent in the Gospels, where the public life narratives are to the fore, but Paul has traces of it in his epistles and picks up at least the last phase of Christ's life in his treatment of Christ's death. In the passage just quoted from 2 Corinthians, Paul rephrases what he said in Philippians 2:6ff. about Christ emptying himself and becoming obedient. Now, however, he describes that emptying as a becoming poor. While the clause "he became poor" refers to the incarnation, it especially embraces, like the Philippians hymn, the death of Jesus. Moreover, Paul uses this description in 2 Corinthians 8 in a context in which he is collecting money for the poor in Jerusalem. Thus, he shows the life of Jesus as embodying social dimensions and strong communal values. The death of Jesus is the final expression of this social dimension of his life. Christ is willing even to die in solidarity with the poor and in persistent commitment to social justice.[5]

> [22]Jews demand signs and Greeks seek wisdom, [23]but we preach Christ crucified, a stumbling block to Jews and folly to Gentiles, [24]but to those who are called, both Jews and Greeks, Christ the power of God and the wisdom of God (1 Cor 1:22-24).

In what we have seen thus far, Christ's life is the rejection of human sin, and his death, therefore, as a confirmation of his life, is the rejection of death as a final confirmation of our separation

---

[5]For further elaboration of this theme, see Leonardo Boff, *Passion of Christ, Passion of the World: The Facts, Their Interpretation and Their Meaning Yesterday and Today* (Maryknoll, N.Y.: Orbis Books, 1987) especially 99–127.

from God. In the mystery of physical death, however, there are also other negative elements which we have seen, such as premature death or violent death, which are seen as *leading to* separation from God rather than *flowing from* such separation. These elements of death may be described more in terms of the mystery of human suffering than the mystery of human sinfulness, but they do point to the totality of death as enemy, as apocalyptic Judaism indicated. Christ's death shows—and makes possible for humanity—not only that death need not be the final confirmation of separation from God, but also that death, even in its enigmatic and threatening dimensions, is not ultimate. Christ not only went to his death as a final act of perfect obedience instead of sin, but he also endured all the mystery and threat of physical death in the sure hope that God would vindicate his trust by ultimately conquering death in all of its spheres.

Paul develops this dimension of the death of Christ in the text cited above from 1 Corinthians. This is a passage that highlights the enigmatic elements of death, labeling it even a stumbling block or a scandal. Paul shows how Christ's life was a puzzle from a human point of view precisely because of his death. To the Jews there was no sign confirming the mission of Jesus as there were signs confirming the prophets; and in fact, his death militated against him because it was a shameful death. Whatever the Jews were expecting as God's final kingdom, it would not in their expectation be brought in by the shameful death of the criminal and a death that expressed failure. Likewise, the Greeks would have made sense of Christ's life if he had used great rhetoric, gathered the elite thinkers of his time, and founded a school of philosophy that would have begun the transformation of the world. But Jesus comes as a poor carpenter, gathers uneducated followers, tells parables, and dies a colossal failure.

Paul says that is the point of God's wisdom. It appears as human folly. Human beings see death as the ultimate failure. They see it as the final expression of human suffering and cannot make sense out of it. Death is enemy because it is mystery and threat as well as because it is final consequence of sin. This, too, Christ conquers. Not only is death not a consequence of sin for Christ, since it is a supreme example of his life of obedience, but his death is not an ultimate threat as suffering, failure, and defeat, since it is experienced in an act of trust that it will be vindicated by God. By thus combining all these dimensions in his death—personal obedience, social justice commitment, trust in suffering—Christ separated physical death from spiritual death and used his own death as a means of atonement for all of us. He made his death a means by which we could conquer sin, separate our own physical death from spiritual death, and eliminate spiritual death from our lives. Christ also sowed the seed by which we could conquer even physical death by not making it the last reality. Christ thus shows how God's justice operates, working actively through the gift of Christ himself to reunite us to God and using even human suffering—that mysterious part of life for which human beings have no adequate explanation—to effectively "make us just."

> I have been crucified with Christ; it is no longer I who live, but Christ who lives in me (Gal 2:20).

In what we have seen God's justice is put in positive light, Christ's death is expiation of sin and not propitiation of God, the cross is not isolated from the rest of Christ's life, and atonement has a social and communal dimension as well as a personal and individual one. The work of Christ is not a penal substitution but a representative journey for all of humanity, enabling us to move from sin to union with God. There remains to discuss one more dimension of this journey in order to complete the picture of how Christ atones for sin.

Thus far we have not elaborated on how Christ's journey becomes participatory. A criticism of the Anselmian theory which we discussed in the introduction of this book is that it accounts for Jesus doing something *for* us and not *with* us. We remain passive recipients. In like fashion, the Anselmian model does not explain how Christ's activities transform us other than by some legal attribution of Christ's "merits" to humanity. The model of the journey seeks to correct these shortcomings. Christians do not receive simply the merits of the journey. Rather, they have the journey itself made available to them in some way. Christ does not live the journey only by himself and for us. Rather, he invites us to live the journey ourselves with him.

Paul expresses such notions in passages such as the one just cited from Galatians. He proclaims that he is with Christ in his cross because he lives with Christ in the resurrection. His life is joined to the life of the risen Christ. In this union he can die to his old way of living and take on the pattern of Christ's life. In doing so, he thus dies with Christ as well as lives with him. Thus, for every Christian, as for Paul, the risen Christ continues to live the pattern of his entire human journey, especially as expressed in his death on the cross, and communicates that pattern for one's own journey. Our own union with Christ is itself a journey because, as we have seen already, the risen life of Christ is not a once-for-all communication but is an ongoing life with a future dimension as well as present. Recall Philippians 3:12, which we studied earlier, and Paul's own stress that he is in process ("I press on"), a point that certainly is not contrary to our model of a journey.

Other texts corroborate this sense of participation with Christ in his death: "As we share abundantly in Christ's sufferings, so through Christ we share abundantly in comfort too" (2 Cor 1:5); "[We] are always carrying in the body the death of Jesus, so that the life of Jesus may also be manifested in our bodies" (2 Cor 4:10). In both these cases we can see a parallel of thought. Whatever Paul says of the resurrection, he says of the death of Christ. Paul's (and every Christian's) share in the death of Christ is of the same intimacy and of the same order as union in the resurrection of Christ, i.e., not just an imitation or resemblance but a genuine sharing in the very life of Christ himself. Further development of this point leads us to consideration of the resurrection of Christ and its importance as part of the saving event, as part of the means of atonement.

Resurrection as Saving Event

If, as we indicated earlier, Paul says in Romans 4:25 that Jesus died for our sins and rose for our justification, then the death and resurrection of Jesus have to be seen as a unity. It would be just as accurate to reverse Paul's phrasing and to say that Jesus died for our justification and rose to save us from sin. In fact Paul does say these things. In Romans 3:24-25 he says that we are justified through Christ's blood (death), a thought repeated in Romans 5:9. In 1 Corinthians 15:17 he says that if Christ has not been raised, we are still in our sins. If we focus on the resurrection aspect of the means of atonement, we must emphasize that it renders Christ's death efficacious in us, i.e., that it makes Christ's death-to-sin and pattern of life present for us in a gradual way whereby these become our journey until we attain the full effects of risen life. In this way, if Christ is not risen, then *his* journey cannot become *our* journey and the cross and death of Christ cannot be efficacious *in us*. To elaborate on this statement we will show two interrelated dimensions of the resurrection of Christ that are often overlooked: first, that resurrection is more than just proof of Christ's saving work, and second, that it involves the total person of Christ, humanity as well as divinity, with implications for our present life as well as for our future.

> [20]Our commonwealth is in heaven, and from it we await a Savior, the Lord Jesus Christ, [21]who will change our lowly body to be like his glorious body, by the power which enables him even to subject all things to himself (Phil 3:20-21).

One of the important aspects of the resurrection of Christ is that it is more than proof of Christ's divinity but is actually a cause of our own transformation. This is not, perhaps, the way in which many Christians were used to considering the resurrection, at least until recently. Even today, many still look upon the resurrection primarily in an apologetic context, using it as a proof of the divinity of Christ. This is the perspective of what I have called "the popular view of the theology of atonement." In this context, resurrection becomes a proof of the atonement worked by Christ. It is not seen, however, as part of the means of atonement itself. According to this view, atonement is worked by the cross, very much on the model of Anselm, and the resurrection is simply a proof *after* the atonement. For Paul, however, the resurrection is neither just a proof of divinity nor just a proof of the atonement, but a transformation of Christ in such a way that the resurrection is an integral part of the saving event itself.[6]

The text we have cited from Philippians shows the customary way for Paul to speak about the risen Christ. In this particular text Paul speaks about future effects. Earlier verses in Philippians 3 and, as we will see later, other texts stress present effects. In either case, the important point is that Christ has entered into his risen life so that he will be able to change us in the same way. Verse 21 says that Christ is in a "glorious body," indicating his risen state and signifying that it is different from our earthly human existence, "our lowly body." We will take that point up again presently. The verse also makes it clear that Christ in that new state is the cause of our own resurrection, for it says that *Christ* "will change us." It also says that he will do so not just by being first example or proof of our own resurrection but by seeing to it that we are "co-formed" (the literal translation of "to be like") to his glorious body. It is by participation in his risen life that we live our new life.

Paul says that Christ does this because he has "power." This power is first of all, as we saw in Romans 1:16, the power of God for salvation. It is the manifestation of God's justice as saving activity. Since God manifests this in Christ, the saving activity is also Christ's power. Now, for Paul, Christ attains this power for salvation above all at his resurrection, for by his resurrection God not only completes Christ's final conquest of sin and death, and not only confirms his obedience unto death, but transforms these into a new risen life that Christ shares with us. We can thus die with Christ and live with him. Resurrection is important not as a proof of atonement, coming after atonement, but as part of the means of atonement itself.

Paul's description of the resurrection as Christ's transformation with power for our salvation is often expressed in terms of Christ's becoming "Lord." The classic text in Paul for this presentation is, of course, Philippians 2:9-11: "[Christ was obedient unto death]. Therefore God has highly exalted him and bestowed on

[6]For a survey of Paul's texts on the resurrection, see Lionel Swain, *The People of the Resurrection: I. The Apostolic Letters* (Wilmington, Del.: Michael Glazier, 1986).

him the name which is above every name, that . . . every tongue confess that Jesus Christ is Lord." There is some debate over whether this title, "Lord," originated for Paul from Greek or Jewish background, but in either case it implies the sharing of Christ in divine powers.[7] This exercise of power is, of course, a share in the general sovereignty of God over all of creation, and it implies the demand for our allegiance through moral uprightness. But part of the exercise of Christ's sovereignty over all of creation is his power to transform us through his risen life.

While it is not explicit in the Philippians hymn, 1 Corinthians 6:11 speaks in this vein about Christ's lordship: "God raised the Lord and will also raise us up by his power." It is difficult to know whether "his" refers to God or to Christ the Lord, but in any case the rest of the passage surrounding this statement gives us the sense of a causal connection between Christ's being raised and ours. We can assume that it is either by Christ's power as Lord or God's power *through Christ's lordship* that we are raised. For the rest of the passage speaks of how we belong to Christ. ("The body [the person] is for the Lord and the Lord for the body" v. 13; "your bodies are members of Christ" v. 15; we are "one spirit with him" v. 17.) Paul is saying in effect that the Christian is *already* participating in the life of Christ. So, it is likely that the completion of one's being in final resurrection is also through union with Christ, who has power as Lord from his own resurrection.

Another text that treats the resurrection not just as proof of divinity but as a transforming power of the risen Christ as Lord is 2 Corinthians 3:18: "We all, with unveiled face, beholding the glory of the Lord, are being changed into his likeness from one degree of glory to another." We will see later that the context around this text speaks of the Spirit's relationship to the risen Christ. Nevertheless, the role of the Spirit is intimately related to the role of Christ as Lord, and this particular verse shows us that openness in faith to Christ's lordship is associated with our transformation into his likeness. We are thereby enabled to see

[7]Reginald H. Fuller, "Lord," in Paul J. Achtemeier, ed., *Harper's Bible Dictionary* (San Francisco: Harper & Row, 1985) 573-574.

God's saving justice not with the partial (veiled) insight of the Old Testament, but with the clear (unveiled) vision of a new revelation. We find here not only the resurrection as part of the means of atonement but also the basis for calling the model of atonement a journey, for our transformation into the risen life of Christ is gradual and ongoing.

To this point we have shown that the means of atonement is the death of Jesus as a representative journey. We have also begun to show, as further means of atonement, that we are invited to participate in that death as part of new life through the resurrection, since the resurrection of Christ is not just a proof of his divinity after his saving work but an empowerment to communicate his life to us. Now we must look with more detail at just how Christ is transformed by the resurrection and just what he communicates to us as life for our participation. The basic point to be made here is that resurrection embraces the humanity as well as the divinity of Christ.

Until recent developments, theology over the past few centuries has been prone to stress the divinity of Christ. While this is not incorrect, it needs nuance, for such a theology does not pay sufficient attention to Christ's humanity and the essential role it plays in atonement. One or two observations will help to introduce this point. First of all, the incarnation is permanent. Once God takes on human existence in Jesus, he never abandons humanity. This applies equally to the risen Christ as to the earthly Jesus. When Jesus rises from the dead, he does not simply "go back to being God." He continues in his human existence, albeit a transformed existence. Secondly, the Christian never perceives Jesus directly as God but always through his humanity. This was the case for the earthly Jesus and continues as the case even for the risen Lord. It was through their experience of the human Jesus transformed in his risen life that the disciples came to see that he was the very revelation of God in our midst.

It is not our concern here to explain how Jesus is God and human, much less to explain his relationship to the Trinity. In fact, such philosophical concerns about the intrinsic being of Jesus are topics for the centuries after the Bible. Our interest here, which is also Paul's concern, is with the functional or practical role of

Jesus for atonement. Our observations lead us to say that however theology eventually comes to explain it, Paul sees only one integrated Jesus, a human being who reveals God and achieves God's work of atonement in our midst. Moreover, there is a transformation of the *humanity* of Christ in the resurrection, so that he reveals God to us in fuller fashion after the resurrection and completes the work of atonement. In other words, for Paul it is not just that *God* is in the humanity of the risen Christ, though that is part of his message, but that God is in the *humanity* of the risen Christ rendering that humanity present for us as our own. Jesus becomes Lord so that his glorified humanity might fully reveal his sharing in divinity, but he becomes Lord also so that his transformed human existence might be present in all time and all ages to transform us and thereby complete the work of atonement. We need now to further elaborate this point in what follows.

Resurrection and the Body of Christ

⁴²So is it with the resurrection of the dead. What is sown is perishable, what is raised is imperishable. ⁴³It is sown in dishonor, it is raised in glory. It is sown in weakness, it is raised in power. ⁴⁴It is sown a physical body, it is raised a spiritual body. If there is a physical body, there is also a spiritual body. ⁴⁵Thus, it is written, "The first man Adam became a living being"; the last Adam became a life-giving spirit (1 Cor 15:42-45).

In his earlier letters Paul simply states the principle that the resurrection is the cause of our own resurrection, the final step of atonement with our total reunion with God. He says, for example, "Since we believe that Jesus died and rose again, even so, through Jesus, God will bring with him those who have fallen asleep" (1 Thess 4:14). In this earliest of his epistles, the apostle intimates that the resurrection becomes the cause of our own resurrection, but he does not yet say how. Is it simply that the resurrection of Jesus indicates the consistent will of God, who will repeat that action in us? Is it simply by setting Jesus up as example of what will happen to us? Is it only a future reality for us after death? Paul answers these questions in his more extensive epistles, showing that our resurrection does not simply follow on Christ's but establishes us in a solidarity with Christ whereby his resurrection becomes the means of our own.

The text above from 1 Corinthians, introducing this section of our study, begins a more elaborate explanation of how this happens. In the first part of 1 Corinthians 15, Paul says that he hands down the good news of the resurrection as part of the early tradition (vv. 3ff.), that denial of the possibility of resurrection would deny the resurrection of Jesus and leave us in our sins (vv. 12ff.), but that indeed Christ has risen from the dead (vv. 20ff.). In the next section (vv. 35ff.) Paul goes on to explain the nature of the resurrection speaking in general terms that include our own resurrection but implicitly treating the nature of Christ's as well. Paul begins by saying that, in fact, one cannot totally explain the resurrection, since it is perceived in faith and since one needs to move to life beyond the grave to experience it in its fullness. Paul says in verses 35-36, "Some one will ask, 'How are the dead raised? With what kind of body do they come?' You foolish man!" This is Paul's way of saying, "You would like me to explain the full nature of the resurrection. Don't ask stupid questions!" Nevertheless, he does attempt to give some insights. What we do know and explain is that dimension of the resurrection which has implications for our life now on this side of death.

The first thing to be said is that resurrection is a change or transformation, the movement from this life into a *new* life, not just the return to this life as one lived it before death. Paul grapples with imagery to say that any resurrection is not the resuscitation of a corpse, a dead body that simply starts breathing again. Resuscitation brings a person back to this world reality and to the human condition experienced in such a world. Resuscitation therefore brings one back to a world of sin and alienation, to all that still needs atonement, and ultimately to the final threat of death once again. Christ was not risen back to that reality, but to a *new* life beyond the climate of sin and death and beyond all the shortcomings of law. The resurrection completed Christ's own journey of perfect obedience and brought him to life perfectly united with God. All this is what Paul is trying to say when he begins his explanation, "What you sow is not the body which is to be, but a bare kernel. . . . God gives it a body as he has chosen" (vv. 37-38). This is Paul's point behind the contrasts such as those given in the text above introducing this section of our study. Finally, the same point is made forcefully in the last part of 1 Corinthians 15 speaking of our own resurrection. Paul says that it may be that the last generation of the final times will not die, but they will necessarily be changed. "Flesh and blood cannot inherit the kingdom of God. . . . We shall not all sleep, but we shall all be changed" (vv. 50–51).

There is, then, a great deal of discontinuity between this life with its death and the new life of resurrection. The risen Christ is different in many respects from the Jesus of history. Nevertheless, there is also much continuity. It is the Jesus who died who is the Jesus who rose. It is we who die who will rise to new life. Moreover, it is the total person who rises, not a disembodied soul. That is why Paul spends time speaking about the resurrection *of the body,* both regarding Christ and ourselves. We must remember, however, what we said previously about Paul's view of human beings. "Body" for Paul usually means the entire person and not just the material or physical part of a human being. When he speaks of the resurrection of the body, he refers to the entire person entering into a new existence. Resurrection of the body should not conjure images of resuscitation, graves opening at the end of time, and corpses being rejoined to souls. Neither does it imply that our risen life will not involve physical dimensions of our being, for we are *enfleshed* spirits, not in two parts but in an inseparable, integrated unity. Resurrection of the body means that *we* who died will move into new life. But we will be changed and how our enfleshed spirit—seen as a totality—will be transformed remains unknown to us. "Lo! I tell you a mystery" (v. 51).

What is said of the resurrection of the body in general is true of the resurrection of Jesus in particular. It is likely that if Paul uses vocabulary involving resurrection and not just immortality of a soul, he intends to involve the entire person of Jesus as an integrated unity. That would include his physical body. But whatever happened to Christ's body, it did not just start breathing again. It takes on a new kind of existence beyond scientific explanation and, indeed, even beyond human imagination. The best we can do to picture the risen body of Christ is to take what we know bodies to be and improve on the image, as if all the resurrection did was give Christ a body of shining light, ease of mobility, and the like. But these are only symbolic images of a radical transformation into a new life for which we have no images. We don't adequately picture the resurrection. We don't scientifically explain it. We believe it and proclaim it for faith. Paul's imagery is to say that the "physical body" becomes a "spiritual body" (v. 44). The risen Christ is neither disembodied nor a resuscitated corpse, but moves from a total human existence limited in its mortal faculties and functions (physical body) to one perfected in final life with God (spiritual body).

In 15:45, Paul moves a step further, for he says Christ is not just a "spiritual body" but a "life-giving spirit." Paul thus makes the point that while descriptions of our resurrection are implicit descriptions of Christ's, nevertheless it is Christ's resurrection that is the principle and the cause of our own. To put this in contemporary theological terminology, Christ, by his resurrection, does not just move to a new human condition in which his conquest of sin and his obedience unto death is brought to new and final union with God. His human life is also transformed in such a way that it is pulled out of the limits of time and space and is able to be present to bring that new life to us in every age and place.

The apostle links this activity of Jesus to the theme of Jesus as the last Adam. He achieves at least two things in doing so. First of all, he transposes a Judaic tradition to make a point about Christ. The tradition is reflected in Philo, but some scholars believe that it had wider circulation in Hellenistic Jewish tradition and that Paul had familiarity with it.[8] According to the tradition, the two creation stories of Genesis were interpreted to give descriptions of two Adams. One was the ideal Adam of the first creation story, made in God's image. The second was the real, historical Adam of the second story, made from the dust and victim of human sin and death. Tradition held that the first was never

[8]C. K. Barrett, *The First Epistle to the Corinthians,* Black's New Testament Commentaries (London: Adam & Charles Black, 1971) 374-375.

more than in the intention of God, while the second was called to become like the first but never did. Paul transposes the tradition. He says the ideal Adam is not the first but the last Adam and that he is not just in the mind of God but a real human person, the risen Christ. Indeed, the Adam of dust has already been surpassed by this last Adam, who reigns in perfect human existence over all sin and death.

Paul makes a second point by his motif of the last Adam. He stresses more thoroughly the solidarity of Christ with all and the transforming power of his humanity. As death came through the first Adam, so life through the last. If the first Adam's sin was more than personal rebellion but created a solidarity in sin to which all humanity has further contributed, so the last Adam lived his life with God for more than himself and created a community of life, which we could share, for union with God. If we recall texts that we have seen, we know that what Paul describes here as future possibility is already begun as present reality. This enlarges the Servant motif that Paul inherited from the traditions before him. Christ's death "for the sins of the many" can now no longer be open to misunderstanding as a representative atonement without our participation. Through the resurrection, Christ is present to us with all that is of enduring value from his life and death, and shares that with us in anticipation of final union with him in the fullness of resurrection.

Resurrection and the Holy Spirit

It is not without importance that Paul has described the risen Christ as being a *spiritual* body and as being a life-giving *spirit*. Paul develops another dimension to the resurrection which complements what we have been saying about Christ, namely, a theology of the Holy Spirit. We turn briefly to this theology.[9]

[17]Now the Lord is the Spirit, and where the Spirit of the Lord is, there is freedom. [18]And we all, with unveiled face, behold-

[9]For a detailed study of this theme see George T. Montague, S.M., *The Holy Spirit: Growth of a Biblical Tradition* (New York: Paulist Press, 1976).

ing the glory of the Lord, are being changed into his likeness
from one degree of glory to another; for this comes from the
Lord who is the Spirit (2 Cor 3:17-18).

This passage is a good place to begin consideration of Paul's view
of the Spirit, for it shows how closely Paul identifies the Spirit
with the risen Lord. Interpretation of this passage is much debated because of the ambiguity of the statement, "the Lord is
the Spirit." The passage is in the context of a comparison between
the Old and the New Testaments. Paul begins 2 Corinthians 3
by commending the Corinthians for opening themselves to the
work of Christ achieved "with the Spirit of the living God" (v. 3),
a work enabling them to live a new covenant not in a written code
but in the Spirit (v. 6). He then illustrates this by new application
of the story of Moses veiling his face so that the people not be
frightened by its radiance and unveiling it when he turned toward
the Lord. Paul says that Moses' veiling his face represents the
incompleteness of the Old Testament (vv. 7-11); his unveiling when
turned toward the Lord represents the fullness of the revelation
when one turns toward Christ and the New Testament (vv. 12-14).

Verses 15-16 introduce our phrase, "the Lord is the Spirit,"
by ending, "When a man turns to the Lord the veil is removed."
Some translate the next clause (v. 17), "Now the Lord is the
Spirit," to mean "Now the Lord of whom this passage speaks
is the Spirit." In this translation "the Lord" does not refer to
Christ at all. The weakness of such interpretation is that in verse
14 Paul says explicitly that Christ removes the veil. Assuming that
"the Lord" refers to Christ, some then translate the clause, "The
Lord is the Spirit," to mean "Christ shows the Spirit in contrast
to the letter of the old covenant." The weakness of this understanding is that it contrasts with the very next clause, where "the
Spirit" must refer to the living person of the Holy Spirit: "Where
the Spirit of the Lord is, there is freedom."

It seems best, then, to say that Paul is making a dynamic connection between the risen Christ and the Holy Spirit in saying that
"the Lord is the Spirit." Once again, he is not trying to define
the ontological and philosophical essence of the risen Lord, or
the inner workings of the Trinity, but only to highlight how closely

the Holy Spirit is related to the risen Christ. Functional theology and the practical realities are to the fore. The living person of the Spirit is so united with the risen Christ that one can say that the Lord is the Spirit. Paul restates this clause again in verse 18 as his way of summing up that the Spirit as well as the Lord frees from the law, enables us clearly to recognize Jesus as Lord, and transforms us gradually into the very likeness of this Lord. What we have been describing as the work of the risen Lord as means of atonement is here attributed to the Spirit as well.

The clues that we gather from this passage in 2 Corinthians help us understand the best approach to take for understanding, according to Paul, the dynamic role of the Spirit in the work of atonement. Perhaps the most important insight is that the Spirit must ultimately always be understood as the Spirit *of Jesus*. It is true that the Spirit is a living person and can be distinguished from Christ. Paul will himself refer to the Spirit often enough as having its own identity. But for all that the Spirit can be *distinguished* from Christ, it cannot be *separated* from Christ. For all that the Spirit is a living person, it shares only one life with Christ and, for that matter, one life in the life of God. While the Spirit is distinguished from Christ or from God the Father, Paul always at least implicitly understands the Spirit as *their Spirit*. He sometimes refers to it explicitly as the Spirit of the Father (1 Thess 4:8: "Whoever disregards this, disregards not man but God, who gives his Holy Spirit to you"; see also 1 Cor 3:16; 6:11; Rom 8:14). Most often, Paul sees the Spirit as shared equally by Jesus, so that it is the Spirit of Jesus (Rom 8:9: "You are in the Spirit, if in fact the Spirit *of God* dwells in you. Any one who does not have the Spirit *of Christ* does not belong to him"; see also Phil 1:19; Gal 4:6).

> [3]No one speaking by the Spirit of God ever says "Jesus be cursed!" and no one can say "Jesus is Lord" except by the Holy Spirit. [4]Now there are varieties of gifts, but the same Spirit. . . . [12]For just as the body is one and has many members, and all the members of the body, though many, are one body, so it is with Christ. . . . [13]And all were made to drink of one Spirit (1 Cor 12:3-13).

If the Spirit is the Spirit *of Jesus,* then we can better understand how the theology of the Holy Spirit is for Paul a complementary dimension of the resurrection of Jesus. If we mean by resurrection that Jesus becomes Lord so that he is now present in every time and every place with new life, another way to say this is that the risen Jesus is now able to pour his Spirit out upon the world in every part and in every generation. If we mean by the lordship of the risen Christ that he is present in order to change us into the likeness of his own transformed human life, which has conquered sin and death, another way to say this is that Jesus gives us his Spirit which thereby recreates us with the very life of Christ. If we have the Spirit of Jesus, we have Jesus, and we can have the Spirit of Jesus because he is not in the past but in the present by virtue of the resurrection.

This is Paul's teaching in the text above from 1 Corinthians 12, where he says that it is only by the Spirit that we can say "Jesus is Lord." When Paul uses the word "say," it is not in the weak sense of bare verbal declamation but implies an acknowledgement with the heart and the experience of Jesus as Lord, i.e., the presence, communication, and empowerment of his human life. In this same chapter from 1 Corinthians, Paul then goes on to speak of the Spirit forming us into the body of Christ. While there is obviously something metaphorical about this concept, Paul intends to capture a reality as well. Recall once again that "body" for Paul means the entire human person, only this time Paul extends the reality to include all human beings as united in the life of Christ. *We* are the body of Christ. In other words, we are no further removed from Christ than Christ is removed from himself. While Christ retains his human identity, the risen body of Christ is of such a nature, pulled out of the limits of time and space, that we can begin to share that same transformed human existence with Christ. His risen humanity continues to live in our humanity. The Spirit of Jesus communicated to us makes us the body or the person of Christ.

Of special interest to us are the communal dimensions of this work of the Spirit of Jesus.[10] Paul does not say that we are the

[10]Jerome Murphy-O'Connor, O.P., *Becoming Human Together: The Pastoral Anthropology of St. Paul,* Good News Studies, vol. 2 (Wilmington, Del.: Michael Glazier, 1982) especially 174–197.

"bodies" of Christ, as if each of us stands in isolation or as if the relationship is only between Christ and each individual. Rather, there is only one body, and in being joined to Christ in one life, human beings are joined to each other in the bond of one shared life. That is why Paul carries out the metaphor of the body by describing the varied members of a body contributing to the good of the entire body. The Spirit thus joins us to Christ in such a way that we are brought into social ties that far surpass the inherently social dimensions of human existence or the mere fact—as philosophers and sociologists might point out—that "no one is an island." In the end, Paul draws on this concept of the body of Christ to challenge the Corinthians to social responsibility, pointing out that all the gifts of the body of Christ are in function of love (1 Cor 13:1ff.). The factions that exist in Corinth (1 Cor 1:10; 3:3; 11:18) are an indication that the work of atonement, begun in the life and death of Christ and made available by his resurrection and gift of the Spirit, have yet to be accepted by the Corinthians in their own lives, especially in their social relationships.

> If the Spirit of him who raised Jesus from the dead dwells in you, he who raised Christ Jesus from the dead will give life to your mortal bodies also through his Spirit which dwells in you (Rom 8:11).

The texts that we have been considering about the Holy Spirit give us indication that the Spirit is not simply a future gift achieving our final resurrection but a present gift beginning the process. In Romans 8 Paul says the Spirit already dwells in us. The Spirit makes present all that is of enduring value in the life of Jesus, in his obedience, and especially in his death, beginning our configuration into Christ in anticipation of the final sharing of the fullness of resurrection. In this verse it is difficult to know whether "his" Spirit speaks of God or Christ, but verses 8–9 show that either description makes sense. Depending on which interpretation is preferred, 8:11 would refer to either the first or the second italicized use of "Spirit" in the following paraphrase, but the *entire* paraphrase captures the full reality implied in the verse:

The *Father gives his Spirit* to Jesus so that the Spirit-empowered Jesus might make his journey through life in the work of atonement until the final conquest of death itself. Then this *Spirit of Jesus* is given to us to work in us what it worked in Jesus, making available to us all Christ's journey of atonement until our own final share in the fullness of resurrection.

In various places Paul gives some further details about our configuration into the life of Christ, showing how we are formed into the body of Christ by the Spirit. He shows that the Spirit gives us, already in our present lives, the ability to *think* as Christ and to *act* as Christ. We will look first at one of the places where Paul speaks directly about the Spirit enabling us to think as Christ.

The Spirit of Wisdom and Action

[11]What person knows a man's thoughts except the spirit of the man which is in him? So also no one comprehends the thoughts of God except the Spirit of God. [12]Now we have received not the spirit of the world, but the Spirit which is from God, that we might understand the gifts bestowed on us by God. . . . [16]"For who has known the mind of the Lord so as to instruct him?" But we have the mind of Christ (1 Cor 2:11-16).

In the first chapters of 1 Corinthians Paul is criticizing the factionalism in that Greek Christian community, a factionalism based on claims by rival groups each saying that they have the better leader and that their version of Christianity gives them a wisdom which the others do not have (1 Cor 1:10ff.). Paul says that Christianity is not based on human wisdom (1:17ff.), that indeed the Corinthian Christians are anything but wise in the estimation of the world (1:26ff.), and that his own preaching in Corinth was not with worldly wisdom (2:1ff.). Then Paul qualifies what he has said, observing that Christians do have a kind of wisdom, though not according to worldly standards, a wisdom revealed through the Spirit (2:6ff.). The apostle describes this as a wisdom "among the mature" (2:6). He is not implying that there are different classes of Christians, with only some entitled to wisdom through the Spirit. All have the potential to become mature. Nevertheless, what the Spirit offers needs to be accepted, and the work of the Spirit in us is gradual. Thus, in this section Paul is going to describe how the Spirit can bring wisdom to those who open themselves to the Spirit's action. This teaching leads us to the verses we have introduced above.

Wisdom is the ability to discern the meaning of life and the prudence to be guided in action by that discernment. Christian wisdom discerns the meaning of life from God's point of view and guides according to God's plan for life. This comes from understanding and then using what God has made available for our lives ("gifts bestowed on us by God," v. 12). Paul explains step by step how this wisdom is acquired, and uses his accustomed anthropological vocabulary. He says human beings know things through their rational faculties or higher powers, their "spirit." God knows through his power or "Spirit" (v. 11). Now God has taken his Spirit and given it to us so that we, possessing his Spirit (v. 12), can know as God knows, at least insofar as we can share as creatures in the divine perspective on our lives. Since the Father shares one life with Christ, then implied behind Paul's words is the fact that the Father's Spirit is also Jesus' Spirit, and we come to a divine perspective by possessing the Spirit of Christ.

In fact, Paul ends this passage by saying that we have "the mind of Christ" (v. 16), i.e., the ability to perceive things from Christ's point of view and thus from God's. Paul uses "mind" in the last verse instead of "Spirit," because he is refuting the Corinthians who are using Isaiah 40:13 in its Septuagint version. The Corinthians are claiming to know the gifts of God and to be above judgment ("Who has known the mind of the Lord so as to instruct him?"), but their wisdom is worldly, self-seeking, and divisive. Paul says, "But *we* have the mind of Christ," the true wisdom that comes as gift through the Spirit. The mind of Christ bringing understanding of the gifts of God comes through the Spirit.[11] We thus have an example of the Spirit enabling us to *think* as Christ, i.e., to see God, God's plan, and God's gifts as does the risen Christ in his transformed human existence.

[11]Charles H. Talbert, *Reading Corinthians: A Literary and Theological Commentary on 1 and 2 Corinthians* (New York: Crossroad, 1987) 5-7.

⁴"We were buried therefore with him by baptism into death, so that as Christ was raised from the dead by the glory of the Father, we too might walk in newness of life. ⁵For if we have been united with him in a death like his, we shall certainly be united with him in a resurrection like his. ⁶We know that our old self was crucified with him so that the sinful body might be destroyed, and we might no longer be enslaved to sin (Rom 6:4-6).

For Paul the Spirit enables us not only to think as Christ but also to act as Christ. There are obviously many passages that would illustrate this point. Anytime Paul gives moral exhortation, it is implicitly founded on conforming oneself to the Lord who lives "in us" (Gal 2:20; Phil 2:5), or on imitating the Lord not just as past example but by imitating others in whom the Lord is present and who already pattern his life (1 Thess 1:6; Phil 3:17). Paul also presumes that it is through the Spirit that this moral activity takes place, for the Spirit operates with activity and power, and not just thoughts (1 Thess 1:5; 1 Cor 2:4), and the Spirit bears fruit in those whom it makes into the likeness of Christ (Gal 5:24). We will not review all these texts but will highlight just one passage which indicates the *start* of this entire process whereby the Spirit enables us to act as Christ, Christian baptism.

The Spirit is not mentioned explicitly in this text from Romans 6, though it may be implied in the reference to Jesus being raised by "the glory" of the Father. (See Rom 8:11, where Jesus is raised by "the Spirit" of the Father.) In any case, Paul does explicitly mention elsewhere that the Spirit is given in baptism (1 Cor 12:13), so that is the implicit background to the text we are considering. The point is that for Paul baptism is the start of one's insertion into the journey of Jesus, so that we do not come *after* Jesus simply to follow his example. In these first verses of Romans 6 as well as in later verses, Paul puts the prefix "with" before several verbs (with-buried, with-crucified, with-live) in order to show the union of the Christian with Christ in all of his activity.

Likewise, for Paul the symbol of baptism is less from the pouring of water than from immersion into it. The being plunged into the water is a symbol of being "buried-with" Christ, being joined with him in his death so as to share one day in the fullness of his risen life. For Paul, what is being symbolized is also happening. Through baptism the Christian celebrates the gift of the Spirit, which begins our conformity to the risen Christ. The transformed human life of Christ is made available as our own. It includes conformity to Christ's death, as that death expresses the death-to-sin and obedience which continues in his risen life. The Spirit enables us to die with Christ to sin and to live with Christ (vv. 10–11) in anticipation of final life in the risen Christ. Thus, the Spirit has us not only think as Christ but act as Christ.

If, indeed, the Spirit enables us to think and act as Christ, then we can say that the Spirit infuses within us the life of Christ as our own life. Paul says this in equivalent fashion when, in Romans 8:16-17, he says that the Spirit is the Spirit of adoption, making us children of God because we are joined to Jesus as son of God: "It is the Spirit himself bearing witness with our spirit that we are children of God, and if children, then heirs, heirs of God and fellow heirs with Christ, provided we suffer with him in order that we may also be glorified with him." (See also Gal 4:6-7). In the last part of this quotation we have also the summary of this chapter of our study. The Spirit is the final aspect of our consideration of the means of atonement. The means of atonement begin when God, with divine justice, sends Jesus to live human life as we all should but do not. Jesus works atonement not by appeasing an angry God but by making a representative journey of obedience, even through suffering and death. The resurrection becomes a necessary means of atonement because it makes Jesus the Lord who is present to all the ages, enabling his human journey to become a participatory journey, to become our journey. The Spirit is the final means of atonement because it is the Spirit of the risen Lord forming us into his likeness, beginning already in the present. By the Spirit we begin our gradual transformation, our journey. The Spirit's infusion reverses sin and alienation, overcomes the destructive powers of law manipulated by sin, and brings us to overcome all forms of death until, finally, physical death itself is overcome and we share in the final glory of the risen Christ.

4

The Goal of Atonement

In the previous chapter we have shown that the popular view of atonement, when it centers on the *means* of atonement, is not supported by Pauline theology. When Paul talks about the means by which Christ reunites us to God, he does not talk of Christ appeasing God's anger or of Christ undergoing the punishment of death as a penal substitute for sinful humanity. Insofar as he talks about the means of Christ's saving work, Paul speaks of the death and resurrection of Christ as saving events into which we are drawn and transformed. If we are going to continue to speak of atonement as the means by which Christ achieves his saving work, then we have to reconceive that definition according to Paul's mind.

It is significant to observe that many scholars do not want to use the word "atonement" when Paul speaks of these means. They prefer to keep Paul's terms like expiation, life in Christ, the gift of the Spirit, or similar vocabulary.[1] We will see that there is some argument for associating these terms with atonement, since they appear around the texts where "atonement" is certainly a suitable translation; but those places where the word "atonement" would most strictly be appropriate in Paul would be where he is describing one end product or effect of Christ's saving activity, and not what I have been describing as the "means." In its root, "atonement" means "being made one" and is another transla-

---

[1]Joseph A. Fitzmyer, S.J., *To Advance the Gospel: New Testament Studies* (New York: Crossroad, 1981) 162–166.

tion of Paul's term *katallagē,* which we translate "reconciliation."
It is in this aspect of its meaning that atonement in the popular
view harmonizes with Paul's vision. We need to look now at those
texts where Paul speaks about reconciliation and its verbal cog-
nate, "to reconcile."

Atonement and the Ministry of Reconciliation

[11]Therefore, knowing the fear of the Lord, we persuade men;
but what we are is known to God. [12]We are . . . giving you
cause to be proud of us, so that you may be able to answer those
who pride themselves on a man's position and not on his
heart. . . . [14a]For the love of Christ controls us, [b]because we
are convinced that one has died for all; [c]therefore all have
died. [15]And he died for all, that those who live might live no
longer for themselves but for him who for their sake died and
was raised.

[16]From now on, therefore, we regard no one from a human
point of view; even though we once regarded Christ from a
human point of view, we regard him thus no longer. [17]Therefore,
if any one is in Christ, he is a new creation; the old has passed
away, behold, the new has come. [18]All this is from God, who
through Christ reconciled us to himself and gave us the ministry of reconciliation; [19]that is, in Christ God was reconciling
the world to himself, not counting their trespasses against them,
and entrusting to us the message of reconciliation. [20]So we are
ambassadors for Christ, God making his appeal through us.
We beseech you on behalf of Christ, be reconciled to God. [21]For
our sake he made him to be sin who knew no sin, so that in
him we might become the righteousness of God (2 Cor 5:11-21).

In sections of 2 Corinthians previous to this text—and, in fact,
as the principal concern of the entire letter—Paul is defending
his ministry to the Corinthians. In earlier chapters he affirms that
his plans, with all their frequent changes, were not a sign of vacil-
lation (1:17) but were the work of God in the risen Christ through
the action of the Spirit (1:21-22). Indeed, Paul's ministry is not
based on the incomplete insights of the Old Testament (3:1-18)
nor on deceptive methods to gain power and a worldly measure

of success (4:1-15). Rather, his ministry is a witness—in action as well as words—of the death and resurrection (4:13-14) which show Jesus as Lord (4:5) and bring life in the Spirit (3:6). Precisely because his ministry is of this sort, Paul is not concerned with worldly power or success and says rather that his ministry entails being conformed to the death of Christ so as to be gradually transformed into the full life of the risen Christ (1:5; 3:18; 4:10).

We recognize in all this, of course, that Paul's ministry is but a sharing with others or a public witness of his own Christian experience and that this experience embraces what we have been calling "the means of atonement" in the previous chapter of our book, though these are understood differently from the way in which the Anselmian or popular view would explain them. Paul's vision of Christianity which he is to share with others is a theology of atonement. In the next section of his letter (4:16-5:10), Paul expresses the desire to be finished with his earthly life but realizes his obligation to please the Lord by the continuance of his ministry. This thought leads to the text which introduces this section of our study, where Paul says that his life in the death and resurrection of Jesus (means of atonement) leads to a ministry of reconciliation (the goal or effect of atonement). We need now to work these verses out more closely.

Paul recapitulates what he has written up to this point in his letter by saying that he stands in good conscience about his ministry (v. 11) and wants to be vindicated in Corinth by the motive for his ministry (v. 12). This motive rests on "the love of Christ" (i.e., Christ's love for us), which shows itself in his death and resurrection (vv. 13-15). Paul is convinced, first of all, that "one has died for all; therefore all have died" (v. 14). The first half of this quotation is a reflection of the early traditional Christian formula that Paul has used elsewhere, when he says, "Christ died for our sins" (1 Cor 15:3). It reflects what we developed previously about the death of Christ on the cross being representative for all humanity and a means of atonement. Paul's accent on universality is also reflected in the phrase "for all." The second half sums up how Christ's representative death affects us. Christ's death does not substitute for our death as if we were not involved;

it invites us to participate with Christ so that we can be said to be dead as well.

The parallel between verse 14b and c and verse 15 elaborates what it means to be dead because Christ died. We can interpret this text in the light of what we developed in our previous chapters. Our dying cannot mean just following Christ into physical death, since "those who live" are the ones who die. Death refers to the kind of death Christ died, an obedient death, in which we can now participate, thus making us dead to our former sinful life. Paul understands this life of sin as "living for self," reminiscent of Adam, whom we saw Paul describing in Romans as disobedient or self-willed (Rom 5:19). Now the death of Christ enables human beings to "live no longer for themselves" but for God through Christ. This, of course, happens when the obedience of Jesus and the quality of his own death endure and become incorporated into his risen life, which he communicates to us for our own. Thus, Paul joins the death to the resurrection: Humans live for Christ "who for their sake died and was raised." These verses recall, then, in succinct fashion, what we previously developed as the means of atonement.

Paul's experience of the death and resurrection of Christ has consequences for himself but also for others. In the next verses Paul speaks of the effects of the death and resurrection of Christ, eventually treating what I have been calling "the goal of atonement," especially reconciliation. The first consequence, which Paul describes for himself—although it can apply equally to every Christian life—is that he no longer regards Christ "from a human point of view" (v. 16). Literally, Paul says that he no longer knows Christ "according to the flesh." Flesh here does not have the negative overtones that we described previously, associated with sin and spiritual death. Its meaning is captured well as "Christ from a human point of view," in contrast to Christ from the perspective of his risen life. Paul is not denigrating the human existence of Jesus, but he is saying that he is not interested in Christ as a historical figure or in Christ as having simply left good teaching from the past or even just good example. The humanity of Jesus is important insofar as it is transformed by resurrection and is made present for Paul and for all.

That this consequence of the death and resurrection is not only for Paul but for all is developed as a second consequence in the following verse 17. Paul also makes more specific that Christ (not "from a human point of view" but as risen Lord) actually enables our participation in his life and thus transforms us: If we are "in Christ," then we are indeed "a new creation." New possibilities are given us "*in* [the risen] Christ," not just "*after* the historical Jesus." Christ is offered not just as good example but as present with transforming power. These possibilities effect changes so radical that they can only be compared to creation beginning again. Obviously, material creation has not disappeared, nor has history been eliminated, so the changes refer to new relationships, to new ways of being, especially for humanity. Whereas we thought and acted in one way in the past, now in Christ we can think and act in new ways. This concept of new creation in Christ helps us see the link between chapters 2 and 3 of our study. The "old" (v. 17) is our sinful way of existence as characterized in chapter 2. We move out of all of that because the risen Christ, as we explained in chapter 3, enables us to exist in new ways that reverse the old: "The new has come" (v. 17).

In verses 18-21, Paul takes these consequences of the death and resurrection of Christ ("All this," v. 18) and describes them as God's work through Christ of reconciliation. What we have been calling "the means of atonement" leads to what we have called "this goal of atonement." Since this effect, which Paul has experienced, is also one which he must proclaim and share with others, then reconciliation can be spoken of as a ministry as well as an experienced effect or goal of Christ's saving work. Thus, Paul uses what seems to be an early Christian credal formula to express this twofold reality; then he repeats each part in expanded form (along with further explanatory notes):[2]

> (a¹) God through Christ reconciled us to himself and
> (b¹) gave us the ministry of reconciliation; (v. 18) that is,
> (a²) in Christ God was reconciling the world to himself, [not
> counting their trespasses against them,]

[2]Ralph P. Martin, *Reconciliation: A Study of Paul's Theology* (Atlanta: John Knox Press, 1981) 92-97.

(b²) and entrusting to us the message of reconciliation (v. 19).
So we are ambassadors for Christ, God making his appeal through us. [We beseech you on behalf of Christ,
be reconciled to God.] (v. 20).

The reconciliation of which Paul speaks is multifaceted. In its
root, *katallagē* means "making otherwise." It refers to a change
from a situation of hostility and alienation to one of friendship
and intimacy. It means basically the restoration of broken relationships, a reuniting of parties that were once separated from
each other. (Hence, the suitability of translating it as "atonement"
in the most proper sense of that word.)

Of course, the primary relationship of which Paul speaks is between God and humanity. If sin, as we saw, is our turning away
from God, leading to death as separation from God, then the
result of atonement as reconciliation is life as union with God,
flowing from minds and hearts united in Christ with God. Notice also that Paul gives the initiative to God. Though he does
not use the same vocabulary, the thought parallels what we ob-
served at the beginning of our study about God's justice. It is a
saving justice, actively engaged on our behalf and not simply a
response to our merits or lack of them. In our text here from
2 Corinthians, Paul says neither that God needs to be reconciled
to us nor that we do the reconciling. God's relationship to humanity is not hostile, though humanity is at odds with God.
Moreover, God does not wait until human beings take the initiative to be reconciled. Therefore, "God reconciles us to himself"
(v. 18).

Paul expands the concept of reconciliation beyond the reuniting of God and humanity. He says that the reconciliation has cosmic dimensions: "God was reconciling the world to himself"
(v. 19). Paul does not elaborate any further in this text on what
he means, and "the world" here could, of course, mean only the
world of human beings. But in Romans 8:19-23, Paul makes clear
that the life in the Spirit, which we described previously, will lead
to a transformation of all of creation itself. The creation was "subjected to futility, not of its own will but by the will of him who
subjected it in hope" (Rom 8:20). Paul presupposes here that the

completion of creation is intimately bound up with human beings, who have stewardship over it. With that background, he says that God allowed creation to be frustrated in its purposes not through its own fault but because of sin. Human beings, in their alienation from God, alienated creation as well from God and from humanity. God, however, allowed this "in hope," i.e., with the plan that human beings reunited with God would also be brought to harmonious union with creation itself and that creation would be "set free from its bondage to decay" (8:21).

In the light of Romans 8, we can say from 2 Corinthians 5:19 that reconciliation is fulfillment of hope for creation, reuniting humanity not only with God but overcoming the hostility among God, humanity, and the world at large. Atonement has cosmic proportions. The place, of course, where this is said most explicitly is in the hymn of Colossians 1:15-20: "[Christ] is the image of the invisible God, the first-born of all creation. . . . For in him all the fullness of God was pleased to dwell, and through him to reconcile to himself all things, whether on earth or in heaven, making peace by the blood of his cross." Whether or not this text is in a letter which we can attribute to Paul, it reflects Paul's ideas, at least as these took shape in the passages we have just seen. This aspect of atonement as reconciliation is a valuable gift in a world threatened by chemicals, nuclear devastation, and other ecological imbalances and is an important contemporary consideration of what Christ's saving work can achieve in our world.

Our treatment of reconciliation is, of course, the description of an ideal. It is only partially attained at present and still remains a future reality. In that regard, atonement achieves its goal in proportion to its means, the risen life of Christ, which has both a present and a future dimension. Yet it is important to recognize that as there is a present power of the risen life of Christ, so there is also reconciliation already achieved and ever-new possibilities for today. Paul expresses these thoughts in the text we have been studying. Though the tense of "reconciling" in verse 19 is ambiguous, Paul says explicitly in verse 18 that reconciliation is a past event already achieved. Nevertheless, it has still to be achieved, for Paul says in verse 20, "Be reconciled." He does not mean here that human beings are to initiate reconciliation, but rather that they are to respond to God's work of reconcilia-tion. Nevertheless, he does indicate that this work of God through Christ is ongoing and still has future dimensions. In this exhor-tation Paul may also implicitly be asking the Corinthians to be reconciled to him as the minister of reconciliation, since the whole point of this letter and the focus on his ministry is to overcome hostility toward him by the Corinthians. If that is the case, then Paul hints at the other dimension of reconciliation, the reuniting of human beings with each other as well as with God and crea-tion. Presently, we will further treat this dimension of reconcilia-tion in a text in Romans 11.

Before moving to this next text, however, we must make one more observation. We mentioned above that there is some argu-ment for using "atonement" to describe what we call "the means" as well as "the goal" of Christ's saving work, provided we un-derstand the means as Paul does. The reason for this is that Paul closely associates the means with the goal. In this text Paul adds what some believe to be a liturgical hymn, but what is in any case a reference to how Christ's death brings about reconciliation. He says, "For our sake he [God] made him [Jesus] to be sin who knew no sin, so that in him we might become the righteousness of God" (v. 21). Some understand this text to mean that Christ was considered a sinner by God so that he might be punished in-stead of us. We have seen that this is not a helpful biblical way of describing Christ's saving work. If we consider Christ as representative, it is so that he might show us how to live a life in perfect unity with God, overcoming sin, death, and law that have dominion in a fallen world (and so that, it is understood, he might communicate such a life to us). Christ "being made sin" would mean that he takes on in his humanity all the effects of the power of sin and death that are possible while still remaining sinless himself ("he knew no sin"), overcomes these effects by his obedience unto death, and thereby enables us to lead a new life conformed to his.

Many scholars also see in this "being made sin" a reference to sacrificial terminology, since the Greek Old Testament and early Christianity used the word "sin" or "for sin" as shorthand for "sin-offering" or "sacrifice for sin."[3] That is not incompatible with the meaning we have just proposed, since, as we have seen, the metaphor of sacrifice does not imply appeasement or penal substitution, but is a particular way of describing the human existence of Jesus and especially his death as in solidarity with sinful humanity in order to reunite us to God. In Romans 8:3 Paul gives evidence that one can understand Jesus "being made sin" in both senses and that they are compatible. There he refers to both the human existence of Jesus in solidarity with sinful humanity and to the life of Christ as a sacrifice: "Sending his own Son in the likeness of sinful flesh [i.e., in solidarity with humanity] and for sin [i.e., as a sacrifice for sin], [God] condemned sin."

From these considerations, then, we see that in the text of 2 Corinthians, where Paul speaks of reconciliation, he also includes mention of the way in which Christ achieves this. "Atonement" in its broadest sense can embrace both the means and the goal of Christ's saving work, though not in the way it has been understood in what I have called "the popular view." One final observation on this text is that to be most accurate, Paul does not associate Christ's sacrifice with reconciliation in verse 21 but with righteousness. That requires our relating righteousness with reconciliation, which we will do under the text of Romans 5. Before that, however, we will give brief treatment to reconciliation in Romans 11.

Atonement as Reconciliation of Humanity

[1]I ask, then, has God rejected his people? By no means! . . . [11]But through their trespass salvation has come to the Gentiles, so as to make Israel jealous. [12]Now if their trespass means riches for the world, and if their failure means riches for the Gentiles, how much more will their full inclusion mean!

[13]Now I am speaking to you Gentiles. Inasmuch then as I am an apostle to the Gentiles, I magnify my ministry [14]in order to make my fellow Jews jealous, and thus save some of them. [15]For

---

[3]Stanislas Lyonnet and Leopold Sabourin, *Sin, Redemption and Sacrifice: A Biblical and Patristic Study,* Analecta Biblica, vol. 48 (Rome: Biblical Institute Press, 1970) 248–256.

if their rejection means the reconciliation of the world, what will their acceptance mean but life from the dead? (Rom 11:1, 11-15).

This passage is in the large context of chapters 9-11, where Paul deals with the relationship between Jews and Gentiles and their place in God's saving work in Christ. In the immediate context of this passage, Paul is dealing with the question of whether the Jews are now abandoned by God because God has worked salvation in Christ among the Gentiles (11:1). His answer is no. God's saving work is to encompass all people. God permitted Israel's rejection of Christ in order to open the gift of salvation to the Gentiles (11:11). (Recall that according to Acts, Paul most frequently preached to the Gentiles of a city only after having been expelled from the synagogue, e.g., Acts 13:42-52; 18:4-7.) Nevertheless, the introduction of the Gentiles to Christ would serve in the long run to entice the Jews also to him. (Paul says also in v. 11, "to make Israel jealous.") The Gentiles ought to appreciate this relationship to the Jews. If the Jews were important even in their initial rejection of Christ, how much more important will they be in their final inclusion in Christ's saving work (v. 12)! These thoughts are essentially repeated in vv. 13-14, with the added thought that Paul saw his own ministry to the Gentiles as part of that plan to entice Israel. He wants to insist that he has not turned his back on his own people, and the implication is that the Gentiles, to whom he is specifically speaking here (v. 13), ought to keep this universal perspective as well.

In the next verse Paul restates the main point about God's universal saving work, but this time in terms of the word "reconciliation," thus bringing us again to the principal object of our study in this chapter. Reconciliation of the world still has the meaning which we described previously of reuniting humanity with God and, perhaps, of restoration of relationships involving creation itself. However, here Paul seems more concerned with the human relationships, especially between Jew and Greek. Could we not, then, see in his statements about reconciliation an implicit statement about restored interhuman relationships? In another "how much more" argument, verse 15 rephrases verse

12 with the vocabulary of reconciliation which we can paraphrase thus: "If the temporary alienation of Israel from God led to reconciliation especially of the Gentiles, how much more will the final acceptance of Israel lead to life from the dead, i.e., to the final consummation of that reconciliation?" That final consummation will be so much more, because it will bring about the reconciliation of the Gentiles not only with God and not only among themselves but with Israel, in a universal unity of all of humanity. If this is the case, then reconciliation is that movement out of sin in all of its social dimensions, as we described it, by being transformed by the risen Christ in such wise that we are drawn into unity with each other in his life.

What we have been finding implicitly in Paul is made explicit in Ephesians 2:11-22. There the author says that the Gentiles, who were alienated from the Jews, have been brought together so that they might be reconciled to God as a unity among themselves. The image he draws is of a new temple (v. 21). In the old Temple there were walls of separation between every group. Gentiles had to remain in the outer court separated from the Jews. We might add that the Jewish women were also separated from the men, and the men from the priests. In Christ, the new temple, the walls are broken down and we are all one. The Letter to the Ephesians may not be Paul's, but this idea grows out of the seed of Paul's thought. Further support for this dimension of reconciliation in Paul can be drawn from his famous dictum in Galatians 3:27-28. There Paul may actually have in mind this same temple imagery, at least for two of his three contrasts, which are identical to what we have just described above: "For as many of you as were baptized into Christ have put on Christ. There is neither Jew nor Greek, there is neither slave nor free, there is neither male nor female; for you are all one in Christ Jesus."

Atonement and Justification

[1]Therefore, since we are justified by faith, we have peace with God through our Lord Jesus Christ. [2]Through him we have obtained access to this grace in which we stand, and we rejoice in our hope of sharing that glory of God. [3]More than that, we

rejoice in our sufferings, knowing that suffering produces endurance, ⁴and endurance produces character, and character produces hope, ⁵and hope does not disappoint us, because God's love has been poured into our hearts through the Holy Spirit which has been given to us.

⁶While we were still weak, at the right time Christ died for the ungodly. ⁷Why, one will hardly die for a righteous man—though perhaps for a good man one will dare even to die. ⁸But God shows his love for us in that while we were yet sinners Christ died for us. ⁹Since, therefore, we are now justified by his blood, much more shall we be saved by him from the wrath of God. ¹⁰For if while we were enemies we were reconciled to God by the death of his Son, much more, now that we are reconciled, shall we be saved by his life. ¹¹Not only so, but we also rejoice in God through our Lord Jesus Christ, through whom we have now received our reconciliation (Rom 5:1-11).

This text in Romans is the centerpiece of Paul's theology of reconciliation. Here Paul brings reconciliation into relationship with other terms, especially with justification. Thus, this passage enables us, on the one hand, to see atonement in its strictest sense of reconciliation as distinct from other descriptions and, on the other hand, to see atonement in its broadest sense of Christ's saving activity as including all of Paul's terms. Before we examine the link between reconciliation and justification we will briefly study the other aspects of reconciliation which either reinforce what we have already seen or contribute new dimensions.

Paul begins this section by saying that we have "peace with God." This term for peace (*eirēnē*) is a relational word and is a synonym for reconciliation, so that Paul can introduce a section on reconciliation by speaking of peace. *Eirēnē* translates the Hebrew word *shalom* and expresses wholeness or fullness of relationship. It is certainly more than the absence of war—when people hold each other at bay simply because they are not strong enough to win a war but continue in feelings of hatred and hostility. Peace is inner harmony, a sense of well-being between peoples. This harmony extends beyond just human relationships. It bespeaks a harmony between God and humanity and a harmony with all of creation as well. True *shalom* exists when one is at peace with self, with God, with neighbor, and with creation itself. One can see that, ultimately, it embraces all the dimensions that we have discussed concerning reconciliation and describes the unity or "at-one-ness" which is the base for our concept of atonement. This peace or reconciliation comes through Christ, showing once again the divine initiative. It is interesting to note Paul's frequent use of "in" or "through Jesus Christ our Lord" in chapters 5–8 and his ending each of these sections of his writings with such a phrasing.

In verse 2, Paul restates in other vocabulary his point about Christ bringing reconciliation. He says that it is through Christ that we "have access to this grace in which we stand," and through Christ that "we rejoice in our hope of sharing the glory of God." Grace is a relational term often associated by Paul with peace (Rom 1:7; 1 Cor 1:3; Gal 1:3). The grace in which we stand is the divine favor obtained through Christ that enables us to approach God no longer in a hostile relationship but in friendship. The word "access" (*prosagōgē*) is used to describe the privilege of an introduction to an important person in society. It builds up the imagery of a new relationship with God that was not the case before because of sin. This new relationship is also called by Paul a "sharing in the glory of God." God's glory is God's exalted nature as it reveals itself and acts in all of creation. When human beings "give glory to God," they are simply affirming this nature of God, associated very much with divine power as well as majesty. For Paul the glory of God includes God's power in raising Christ from the dead (Rom 6:4) so that Christ might become himself the "Lord of glory" (1 Cor 2:8) and show God's power by bringing us to new life conformed to his "glorious body" (Phil 3:21). Without Christ, of course, we "fall short of the glory of God" (Rom 3:23).

When Paul rejoices in sharing in the glory of God, he describes it as "our hope," indicating that the final sharing in the risen life of Christ is still in the future. Nevertheless, we begin that sharing already. In our treatment of the gift of the Holy Spirit as part of the means of atonement, we mentioned that through the Spirit we are all "being changed into [Christ's] likeness from one degree of glory to another" (2 Cor 3:18). Thus, whether it be described as reconciliation or in some equivalent way as "having peace," "obtaining access," or "sharing in glory," this goal of atonement is both a present and a future reality, achieved on God's initiative through the death and resurrection of Christ and the gift of the Spirit.

As Paul continues in this passage in Romans 5, he makes explicit reference to God's initiative and to the means of atonement as we described them in the previous chapter. Paul says his confidence in the availability of reconciliation is firm even in the midst of suffering because the foundation of it all is the love of God shown in the gift of the Spirit. The Greek phrase *hē agapē tou theou* ("the love of God") in verse 5 can mean our love for God or God's love for us. The translation we have used, "God's love," is the better, since the rest of the verse tells of what God has offered us. Moreover, the next verses make the point that we merited nothing and took no initiatives but that God reached out to us in our sinfulness. Thus we have God's love as active and saving, reminiscent of our earlier development of God's justice as saving activity and as taking the initiative. Mention of the Spirit recalls what we developed in chapter 3 about the means of atonement. It is the Spirit who transforms us gradually into the likeness of Christ so that we may have peace and be reconciled. That God's activity is performed with generosity and great care for us is indicated by Paul's saying that God's love is "poured" into our hearts. This term may also be an allusion to the blood of sin-sacrifice "poured" on the altar, an anticipation of the following verses that show how God's love is manifest especially in the sacrifice of Christ.

Beginning with verse 6, Paul elaborates more fully on the means of reconciliation, supporting our earlier suggestion that atonement in its broadest sense should embrace the means as well as the goal of Christ's saving work. God's initiative is shown in the death and the resurrection of Christ. We have already considered Romans 5:7-9, when we showed that Christ in death was not as a penal substitute but more in the mode of the righteous martyr and in the pattern of a sacrificial offering to reunite us to God. This pattern seems especially indicated by the mention of Christ's "blood" (v. 9) as well as his "death" (v. 10) to reconcile us. Moreover, the introduction of "the wrath of God" (v. 9) should not cast doubt on this claim. We have seen that the wrath of God is a technical term in Paul, far removed from any sense of vindictive anger and much different from God's justice as saving activity. While sin must be shown as totally incompatible with God, God requires no appeasement but rather actively seeks to eradicate sin through Christ's death. The blood of Christ symbolizes life returning to God, and the death of Christ represents his life of perfect obedience to God. The death of Christ is joined to his resurrection, so that Paul can assert, "Much more now that we are reconciled [by the death], shall we be saved by his [risen] life" (v. 10). Once again, Paul indicates a future reality, but we have seen that there are also present dimensions to this saving work of Christ. (See also 2 Corinthians 6:2: "Now is the day of salvation.")

Having elaborated once again what I describe as "the means of atonement," Paul then returns in verses 10-11 to the goal or effect of this saving work, namely, reconciliation. Notice again how Paul does not say that God was enemy to us but that we were enemies to God, and that it was through divine initiative that we were reconciled. Notice also that Paul treats reconciliation as an already accomplished event, although we know from earlier analysis that he also acknowledges a dimension yet to be achieved. Our insertion into the risen life of Christ is an ongoing process. In any case, reconciliation seems to be the high point of this passage of Romans, and it is now time to ask just how significant reconciliation is in the overall theology of Paul. In doing so, we will also consider the relationship of reconciliation to other terms, especially "justification," thus sketching a fuller picture of Paul's theology of atonement in its broadest sense.

There is much validity behind the observation that Paul uses many different terms to describe Christ's saving activity in our lives and that each term must be considered on its own. "Reconciliation" should not be made identical with "justification" or "justification" with "redemption," etc. Each word captures a slightly different nuance. Nevertheless, there is some merit in relating the terms to each other, for this comparison may help to discern an accent or emphasis in Paul's overall vision. We will compare "reconciliation" and "justification" as two of the principal images used by Paul. The analysis which follows can be described only as tentative. Its results are surprising at first glance. "Justification" is the term used most frequently by Paul to describe Christ's work, and "reconciliation" is hardly used at all. Yet, reconciliation may be more at the center of Paul's thought than justification. This conclusion is disputed by many scholars who think Paul's centerpiece is justification by faith.[4] Nevertheless, there is some support in Paul's writings for this claim, and so, with this caution, we proceed with our analysis.

Two facts give credibility to the importance of reconciliation for Paul: the location of Romans 5:1-11 in the overall thought of the epistle and the way in which "justification" and "reconciliation" are grammatically related in the few texts where reconciliation is mentioned by Paul. First of all, an outline of Romans shows that 5:1-11 is a key transition passage between major sections. This text gathers up the thought of Romans 1-4 with its concentration on wrath, ungodliness, and justification and shows that these early chapters are in function of further activity, which will be treated in the following chapters, especially chapter 8. This further activity will be described in more personal and relational themes, such as life in Christ and especially the powerful working of the Spirit, so Paul introduces these themes with the relational imagery of peace or reconciliation. Thus, "reconciliation," while not used extensively, appears as a pivotal term in the letter, and "justification" seems to be in function of reconciliation. Given the fact that Romans is also the closest we come to a synthesis of Paul's vision of Christianity, then reconciliation seems not only central to Romans, but also a good way of summing up Paul's theological vision.

The grammatical relationship of "reconciliation" and "justification" is also of interest. In the few passages where Paul uses the term "reconciliation," the word "justification" or "justify" is put into a subordinate position, indicating that "justification"

[4]See Fitzmyer's observations on Käsemann's claim that justification is central, Fitzmyer, *To Advance the Gospel,* 170-173.

is in view of something else, namely, reconciliation. Thus, "being justified" is a participle subordinate to the main verb: "Since we are justified [literally, having been justified] by faith, we have peace" (Rom 5:1). In the passage we saw previously from 2 Corinthians 5:19, Paul puts the concept of justification in a clause subordinate to his main thought about the ministry of reconciliation: "God was reconciling the world to himself, not counting their trespasses against them." It is possible also that in the later verse 21 of this same text, Paul incorporates a liturgical piece about justification precisely in order to explain reconciliation as the final effect of Christ's sacrifice which leads to justification. Certainly in the context around this verse the main topic is reconciliation and not justification.

While these arguments do not remove all doubt about the relationship of reconciliation to justification, they do indicate that reconciliation is more important to Paul than his infrequent use of the term might indicate. If the arguments have validity, then Paul's vision of Christianity is a theology of atonement in the strictest sense of the term as the process leading to reconciliation of the world. If, on the other hand, reconciliation is not for Paul a summary of all of Christ's saving work but simply one of many terms, then we can say that Paul's vision of Christianity is a theology of atonement in the broadest sense of the word, incorporating both reconciliation and justification as well as other concepts. In either case, we ought to conclude our discussion of Romans 5:1-11 with a brief description of the meaning of justification.[5]

From our discussion of the justice of God, we have already had some introduction to the meaning of justification (the noun *dikaiosynē*) and to God's justifying persons (the verb *dikaioō*). The terms reflect what is manifested by God's justice, the effects in us when the justice of God is seen as an objective genitive or as gift. As a metaphor, justification is a judicial or forensic term and indicates God's verdict of acquittal on human beings guilty of sin. (Recall 2 Corinthians 5:19: "not counting their trespasses against them.") However, while not losing its legal connotation,

---

[5]For a detailed study of justification see John Reumann, *Righteousness in the New Testament* (Philadelphia: Fortress Press, and New York: Paulist Press, 1982).

the term also embraces relational dimensions. As God's justice is God's fidelity to covenant, so justification or his justifying action is the reestablishment of human beings in their proper relationship to God within the covenant. Keeping the legal context, we may say that people are not just pronounced innocent but are reestablished in right relationships.

Paul finds this forensic way of talking about Christ's saving work especially when, in the forensic debates raised by opponents over the role of law, he is arguing for the gratuity of God's action in Christ and its acquisition through faith and not by any works of the law. (See Gal 3:11; Rom 3:21; it is also the point of the entire chapter of Romans 4.) God declares us just not because of or by our keeping of the law but through our union with Christ in his death and resurrection. This leads to an appreciation of atonement in Christ as countering law as well as sin and death. We have seen in chapter 2 that while law is good, it has inbuilt shortcomings and that we cannot in the long run keep the law. Justification is Paul's way of saying that God rights the wrongs, but goes another route than through the law. On the one hand this means that through Christ "the just requirements of the law might be fulfilled" (Rom 8:4) without the shortcomings ("what the law weakened by the flesh could not do" Rom 8:3). On the other hand this means that Christ frees us from the law, because he enables our living through the inner power of the Spirit and not because of the demands of law. (Thus, in Gal 3:10-14, in saying that Christ absorbs the curse of the law, Paul uses rabbinic argumentation in finding new application for an Old Testament text: Christ, in being condemned to death, took all the legal sanctions that law could exact according to Deut 21:23, and so "exhausted" the role of law to condemn us without being able to change us. This opened the way for life in the Spirit through faith.)

From what we have said about justification being a relational as well as a juridical concept, we should appreciate one final dimension to this effect of Christ's atonement in the broad sense of the term. Justification is not simply an extrinsic declaration of innocence, as if God considers a person not guilty although he or she still is. Rather, the God who declares justice also constitutes persons in justice. We may say that, ultimately, justification or righteousness has an ethical dimension as well as a forensic one, and that one who is justified now has the ability to begin living a new life in Christ. Thus, in Romans 5:19 Paul says literally that the Christians are "constituted" (*katastathēsontai*) righteous. In Romans 8:10, the righteous are said to be alive through the Spirit of Christ. Recall also the phrasing of 2 Corinthians 5:21, which says that we "become" the very righteousness of God in Christ.

Atonement and Redemption

Justification expands the mosaic of the effects of Christ's saving work and enlarges our picture of atonement in the broad sense of that word. It also builds on what we described as the means of atonement in the previous chapter. Paul uses other metaphors to describe the effects of Christ's saving work, but we do not have space to analyze them here.[6] However, we conclude this book with a brief reference to one other metaphor that Paul uses, that of redemption, because it is important in the popular view of atonement and is at variance with Paul's understanding (Rom 3:24; 8:23; 1 Cor 1:30). In the popular view derived in part from Anselm, redemption is often conceived as a price that Christ pays to God in order to save us. This price is his life offered instead of our lives. It was this concept of redemption that became attached to atonement, was joined to a theory of sacrifice as penal substitution, and led to much of the explanation of atonement described in the introduction to this book as Christ "making up" to God for our sins.

Some observations will show that this explanation of redemption is not Paul's.[7] First of all, redemption does have the idea of a buying back or liberation, and it has some similarity to the practice in Paul's time of slaves purchasing their freedom from

---

[6]For an analysis of Paul's vocabulary on Christ's saving work, see Joseph A. Fitzmyer, *Paul and His Theology: A Brief Sketch*, 2nd ed. (Englewood Cliffs, N.J.: Prentice-Hall, 1989) 59–71.

[7]Lyonnet and Sabourin, *Sin, Redemption and Sacrifice*, 79–119.

their owners through a religiously symbolic gesture of leaving the money before a god, as if the god purchased the slave. However, the similarity is only general, since for Paul we had no means to purchase our own freedom as the slaves had, since Christ purchased us slaves really and not through a fictive gesture, and since Paul never indicates to whom a price was paid. The idea of redemption needs to be modified by Old Testament data in which the "redeemer" was one of the kinsfolk who came to the rescue by buying back the lost freedom of a relative in debt. Thus, God is like a close relative, actively interested in securing our freedom, not being paid or appeased but through Christ bringing about our deliverance. The Old Testament rarely speaks of ransom prices being paid to anyone.

Moreover, the Old Testament also associates God's redemptive work with the idea of acquisition. Redemption means that God through Christ has acquired us as God's own possession. When Paul says, therefore, "You were bought with a price" (1 Cor 6:20; 7:23), he means that it cost Christ a great deal or that the love of God went to great lengths to acquire us for divine possession, but it does not mean that Christ paid a price to God or had to appease God for us. This idea of redemption as we have been analyzing it is joined, in Romans 3:24-25, to the idea of sacrifice as expiation as we outlined it in chapter 3 of this study. This reinforces the insight that redemption is not Christ's paying the price of appeasement as penal substitute but is Christ's work of reacquiring, rededicating, and reuniting us to God. Thus, redemption can be joined to reconciliation and to justification as description of the goal of atonement, and it does not militate against the consistent picture of Christ's death being joined to his resurrection as the means of all those effects of atonement.

This completes the picture of Paul's vision of Christianity as atonement. In its strictest sense this means the goal of Christ's work of reconciliation, a description compatible with the popular view of atonement as well. In the broadest sense of the word, Paul's vision is of atonement as embracing justification and redemption as well as reconciliation and, as it also describes the means of this saving work, Christ's death and resurrection and the gift of the Spirit. In this regard, it does necessitate a change in the way the Anselmian and the related popular view of atonement see redemption and the sacrificial means of Christ's death as penal substitute. We are not saved if Christ only does something *for* us. God's justice has impelled him in love to give us the death and resurrection of Christ as our own journey, to be lived *with* Christ until we are fully justified and redeemed and especially until we are fully reconciled, both individually and communally, in a union with God, self, neighbor, and creation itself.

Suggestions for Further Reading

Boff, Leonardo. *Passion of Christ, Passion of the World: The Facts, Their Interpretation, and Their Meaning Yesterday and Today.* Maryknoll, N.Y.: Orbis Books, 1987.

Byrne, Brendan, S.J. *Reckoning with Romans: A Contemporary Reading of Paul's Gospel.* Wilmington: Michael Glazier, 1986.

Daly, Robert J., S.J. *The Origins of the Christian Doctrine of Sacrifice.* Philadelphia: Fortress Press, 1978.

Fitzmyer, Joseph A., S.J. "Reconciliation in Pauline Theology." *To Advance the Gospel: New Testament Studies.* New York: Crossroad, 1981.

Lyonnet, Stanislas, S.J. and Leopold Sabourin, S.J. *Sin, Redemption and Sacrifice: A Biblical and Patristic Study.* Analecta Biblica, vol. 48. Rome: Biblical Institute Press, 1970.

Martin, Ralph P. *Reconciliation: A Study of Paul's Theology.* Atlanta: John Knox Press, 1981.

Morris, Leon. *The Atonement: Its Meaning and Significance.* Downers Grove, Ill.: Inter-Varsity Press, 1983.